The
Editor's Guide *101*
For Indie Authors

Discipleship Press

Website: www.discipleshippress.wordpress.com
Email: maluthabiel@gmail.com
Phone: +254 797 624 994

~~***~~

P.O. Box 28448-00100, Nairobi Kenya

Library of Congress Control Number: 2022907954

CONTENTS

CHAPTER 10: FORMATTING AS PART OF EDITING (BECAUSE LAYOUT CREATES NEW ERRORS)...128

CHAPTER 11: COVER AND BOOK PACKAGING (EDITING THE FIRST IMPRESSION) 142

DEDICATION

To the indie author who refuses to publish a book that feels
rushed.
To the patient reader who deserves clean pages.
To every editor, beta reader, and honest friend who told me, "This
part is not clear," and helped me grow.

AUTHOR'S NOTE

I wrote this guide because I have seen the same pattern repeat for years. A writer finishes a draft, feels the rush of victory, and then publishes too fast. Later, reviews mention confusion, repeated lines, weak flow, or errors that could have been caught with a steady process. The painful part is this: most of those problems are not talent problems. They are process problems.

Editing is not the stage where you "fix a few commas." It is where you protect your reader. It is where you protect your name. It is where you turn a private draft into a public product. If you are indie publishing, you do not have a traditional publishing house catching what you missed. That is why your editing system matters.

In this book, I teach editing in a way that respects two realities at the same time: quality is non-negotiable, and most authors have limited time and money. I will show you how I edit in passes, what to do first, what to do last, what to hire out, and what you can do yourself with discipline. My goal is simple. When you press publish, you should feel peace, not fear.

HOW TO USE THIS BOOK

This guide is built for action. I recommend you use it in a working way, not as something you only read once.

1) Start with one manuscript.
Pick the book you are editing right now. Do not try to apply everything to five projects at once. One book, one system, one finish.

2) Edit in passes, not in panic.
Most writers mix everything together. They rewrite a sentence, then correct punctuation, then rethink the chapter structure, then change the title, then doubt the whole book. That is how editing becomes exhausting. I will lead you through clean passes so you focus on one type of problem at a time.

3) Use the chapters as a checklist in order.

- Chapters 1–4 reset how you think about editing and genre expectations.
- Chapters 5–9 give you my workflow, feedback systems, and tool discipline.
- Chapters 10–13 help you avoid layout errors, packaging mistakes, and last-minute surprises.

4) Decide early if you are hiring an editor.
If you plan to hire help, read Chapter 6 and Chapter 7 sooner rather than later. It will save you money and confusion. If you are editing alone, the self-editing method in Chapter 5 becomes your main path.

5) Keep a simple editing notebook.
As you work, write down recurring issues you notice in your writing. Repeated words, unclear transitions, weak openings, tense shifts, character name spelling, citation habits, anything. That notebook becomes your personal quality tracker.

6) Do the practice sections.
Each chapter includes a practical exercise. Do not skip them. The book becomes far more useful when you build your own templates, checklists, and habits from it.

INTRODUCTION

When I first started taking publishing seriously, I thought editing was the last step. I believed the real work was writing, and editing was a quick cleanup before release. That belief cost me time, reputation, and confidence.

I learned that editing is the real gate between intention and impact. A draft can have a powerful message, a strong story, or a valuable lesson, and still fail the reader because it is not clear enough, not organized enough, or not consistent enough. Readers do not see your effort. They see what is on the page.

This book is my practical answer to one question: How do I produce a professional book as an indie author, without guessing?

You will learn the levels of editing, the order they should happen in, and the specific moves that make your manuscript cleaner and stronger. You will learn how to protect your voice while removing what weakens it. You will also learn how formatting and cover choices create trust, and why a final proof after layout is not optional.

By the end, you should be able to look at your manuscript and say, "I know what to fix first. I know how to fix it. I know when I am done."

CHAPTER 1: WHAT EDITING REALLY IS (AND WHY IT EXISTS)

Editing is not punishment. Editing is not proof that I failed. Editing is not the boring step I rush through before I reward myself with publishing.

Editing is where a manuscript becomes a book.

When I say "book," I mean something different from "draft." A draft is a private thing. It is my mind speaking to itself. A book is public. A book makes promises to strangers. A book enters the marketplace of attention where readers spend their limited time, money, and trust. Editing is the bridge between those two worlds.

I once believed editing meant correcting mistakes. I thought of it as sweeping a room after a party, picking up broken cups, and hiding the mess. But the deeper I went into publishing, the more I realized editing is closer to construction than cleaning. It is not just about removing errors. It is about shaping meaning so the reader receives what I intend, without confusion or distraction.

Editing Is Bigger Than Grammar

Grammar matters, but grammar is not the whole house. Grammar is the paint and the polish. The house itself is clarity, structure, consistency, and trust.

1) Clarity

Clarity means the reader understands what I mean the first time they read it. They do not have to reread a sentence three times. They do not have to guess who is speaking. They do not have to translate my thoughts into their own language.

Clarity is also moral. It is respect.

When I write a confusing paragraph, I am asking the reader to do extra work that is not their job. It is my job. Clarity is me paying my debt to the reader.

Clarity is not dumbing down. Clarity is discipline. It is choosing the strongest words, the cleanest sentences, and the simplest path to the point. Even complex ideas can be written clearly. In fact, complex ideas demand clear writing more than anything else, because confusion multiplies quickly.

If I want to measure clarity, I ask simple questions:

- Can a reader summarize this paragraph in one sentence?
- Is the subject of each sentence obvious?
- Do my pronouns point to clear nouns?
- Did I introduce an idea before I started using it?
- Is my meaning hidden behind abstract words?

A sentence can be grammatically correct and still unclear. Editing teaches me that correctness is not the same as communication.

2) Structure

Structure is the order of ideas. It is the sequence of scenes. It is the skeleton that makes the body stand.

Many writers try to fix a structural problem with better sentences. That is like trying to fix a crooked wall by painting it again. It may look better for a moment, but the building is still unstable.

Structure answers questions like:

- Does this chapter have a purpose?
- Does each section move the reader forward?
- Does my argument build logically?

- Does the story rise and fall with intention?
- Are my transitions strong enough to carry the reader?

When structure is weak, readers feel it as boredom, confusion, or fatigue. They may not be able to explain what is wrong, but they feel it. Editing exists because structure is rarely perfect in the first draft. The first draft is often a discovery journey. I write to find what I really want to say. Editing is where I decide the best way to say it.

3) Consistency

Consistency is the quiet discipline that makes a book feel professional. It is the part many readers never praise, but they punish when it is missing.

Consistency includes:

- Names and spellings
- Timeline and sequence
- Point of view and tense
- Tone and voice
- Terminology and definitions
- Formatting and style choices

A book can have strong content and still feel sloppy if it is inconsistent. If a character's name changes spelling, the reader starts doubting everything. If my tone shifts without reason, the reader stops trusting the narrator. If my key terms change, the reader wonders whether the writer knows what they are doing.

Consistency is not only technical. It is emotional. It tells the reader: "You are safe here. I will not waste your time. I will not confuse you."

4) Reader Trust

Reader trust is the currency of publishing. Once it is lost, it is hard to regain.

Trust is built when I keep my promises. The promises begin at the cover, continue through the title, and then intensify on the first page. If I promise a practical guide, I cannot give a sermon. If I promise a thriller, I cannot deliver a slow philosophical walk with no tension. If I promise a memoir, I cannot sound like a marketing brochure.

Editing protects trust by asking the hard questions:

- Am I delivering what I promised?
- Is my voice honest?
- Are my claims supported, or are they exaggerations?
- Have I earned the emotional moments, or did I force them?
- Does this book feel like a finished product?

If I care about publishing, I must care about trust. Editing is how I show that care.

Why Editing Exists: A Short History of an Old Discipline

Editing did not begin with self-publishing. It did not begin with modern publishing houses. Editing exists because human communication is imperfect and writing is harder than it looks.

Even in older societies, people revised speeches, corrected manuscripts, and refined texts before passing them on. Whenever writing became public, it needed correction. Scribes copied texts by hand. Copying created errors. Those errors had consequences. If a religious text, law, or historical account had mistakes, it could mislead a community. That is why careful copying and correction became a serious practice.

Later, when printing technology arrived, the stakes increased. A single mistake could be multiplied across thousands of copies. Printing did not remove errors. It multiplied them. That reality made editing even more important. The more books were produced, the more the industry needed systems to prevent permanent mistakes.

Traditional publishing developed layers of quality control because it had to. It was selling products, and products must meet standards. Editors existed to protect the publisher's reputation, protect the author's work, and protect the reader's experience.

Now, indie publishing has changed the gatekeeping, not the need for editing. The gate is open, but the reader's expectations did not become lower. In some categories, expectations became higher because readers can compare books instantly. They can download a sample in seconds. They can leave reviews publicly. They can warn others.

This is why modern indie publishing makes editing unavoidable. In the past, an author could sometimes rely on the publisher's process. Now, the author is the publisher, or the author becomes the manager of a small production team. That means I must either build a personal editing system, or I must pay for professionals, or I must do a wise combination of both.

Indie publishing is freedom, but freedom is not a free pass. Freedom is responsibility.

Why Editing Feels Painful

Editing feels painful because it attacks my identity. Writing is personal. Even nonfiction carries my voice. When I see a weak sentence, it can feel like I am weak. When someone points out a flaw, it can feel like they are pointing at me.

But editing is not judgment of my worth. It is judgment of the manuscript as a product and as a message.

There is another reason editing hurts. Writing is often emotional. A first draft holds energy, anger, love, and desire. Editing forces me to slow down and look at the work with cold eyes. It requires discipline. Discipline always feels heavy at first.

Yet the pain has a purpose. It trains me to separate myself from the manuscript, so I can improve it. This separation is not emotional death. It is maturity.

When I accept editing, I accept growth.

My Draft Reality Principle

One of the most important lessons I ever learned in publishing is this:

The first draft is raw material, not a finished product.

This principle saved me from unrealistic expectations. It saved me from self-hate. It saved me from publishing too early.

Raw material is valuable, but raw material is not ready. A tree can be strong, but it is not a table until it is cut, shaped, sanded, and finished. A stone can be precious, but it is not a ring until it is polished and set.

A first draft is often a bag of potential. It contains the story, the message, the heart, and the voice. But it also contains repetition, confusion, filler, unnecessary scenes, and unclear arguments. It contains emotional writing that needs shaping. It contains content that belongs in the author's journal, not in the reader's book.

The draft reality principle gives me patience. It reminds me that the first draft does not have to impress anyone. The first draft has one job: to exist.

Then editing begins.

When I forget this principle, I expect my first draft to be clean. I expect it to be powerful. I expect it to be perfect. Those expectations lead to disappointment. Disappointment leads to quitting. Quitting leads to unfinished books.

When I remember this principle, I relax. I write freely, knowing I will refine later. Editing becomes my partner, not my enemy.

What Editing Does for Me as an Indie Publisher

As an indie publisher, editing does not only improve the manuscript. It also improves my long-term career.

It protects my name

Indie publishing is built on catalog growth. Each book becomes part of my permanent record. If I publish sloppy books, I train my audience to expect sloppiness. If I publish clean books, I train my audience to trust me.

Trust compounds. So does distrust.

It protects my future sales

A clean book gets better reviews. Better reviews lead to more sales. More sales lead to more visibility. Editing is not only artistic. It is also business.

It protects my time

Mistakes cost time. A published book with errors leads to updates, complaints, refunds, and reputation repair. A careful edit saves time because it prevents messy consequences.

It trains my craft

Every edit is a lesson. Editing teaches me what my weaknesses are. It shows me patterns. It exposes habits. It teaches me how to write better drafts next time. Editing is education.

The Four Big Questions I Ask When I Edit

Whenever I open a manuscript, I bring four questions. They guide me more than any tool.

1) What is this trying to be?

Genre, promise, audience. If I do not answer this, my edit becomes random.

2) Does it succeed at being that?

Does it deliver on what it claims? If not, what must change?

3) What is weakening it?

Confusion, repetition, weak structure, inconsistent voice, sloppy mechanics.

4) What is the simplest path to fix it?

Not the fanciest solution. Not the solution that makes me feel smart. The simplest path that improves the reader's experience.

These four questions keep editing grounded.

Practice Section: My 30-Minute Manuscript Diagnosis (Quick Self-Audit)

This is one of the most useful habits I have ever built. Before I do deep editing, I do a fast diagnosis. I do not fix anything yet. I only look for patterns and decide what kind of work this manuscript needs.

I set a timer for 30 minutes. I keep a notebook or a document open for notes. I move quickly.

Minute 1–5: The Promise Test

I read:

- The title (or working title)
- The subtitle (if nonfiction)
- The back cover blurb or description (even if rough)
- The first page

Then I ask:

- What does this promise the reader?
- Does the first page match that promise?
- Is the voice consistent with the promise?

If the promise is unclear, the edit will be messy. I fix the promise first, even if it is only a private statement. I write one sentence: "This book helps the reader do ___."

Minute 6–12: The Structure Scan

I look at:

- The table of contents or chapter list
- Headings inside two random chapters
- The opening and ending of one chapter

Then I ask:

- Does each chapter have a clear job?
- Are chapters repeating the same message?
- Are there missing steps or missing scenes?
- Do transitions exist, or does the book jump?

I do not try to perfect the structure in these minutes. I only identify whether structure is the biggest problem or not.

Minute 13–18: The Clarity Check

I pick one section, about two to three pages, and I read it out loud, quietly if needed.

Out loud reading exposes what silent reading hides. I listen for:

- Long sentences that collapse under their own weight
- Confusing pronouns
- Abstract language without concrete meaning
- Jargon without definition
- Places where I stumble while reading

Every stumble is a signal. If I stumble, the reader will stumble.

I note the common issues. If the problem is clarity, I will do a line edit pass later.

Minute 19–24: The Consistency Sweep

In these minutes, I scan for:

- Name spellings
- Capitalization choices
- Repeated words and phrases
- Tense shifts
- Point-of-view shifts

- Formatting inconsistencies

I do not fix them yet. I only mark patterns.

Consistency problems are often easy to fix once I have a style sheet. The purpose of this sweep is to see whether I need that style sheet urgently.

Minute 25–30: The Trust Score

Now I answer honestly:

- If I were a stranger, would I keep reading?
- Does this feel professional, or does it feel like a draft?
- What are the top three issues that damage trust?

Then I write a simple plan:

My top 3 issues:

1. _____
2. _____
3. _____

My next pass:
I will do a ____ edit pass first, because ____.

That is it.

This 30-minute diagnosis stops me from editing blindly. It prevents me from wasting hours polishing sentences in a chapter that should be cut or reordered. It helps me act like a publisher, not only a writer.

Closing Thought for Chapter 1

Editing exists because writing is human. Humans repeat themselves. Humans forget what they already said. Humans assume others know what they know. Humans rush. Humans get emotional. Humans get tired.

Editing is the discipline that corrects human weaknesses so the reader receives a clean experience.

When I accept editing, I accept the truth: my draft is not my book yet. My draft is the raw clay. Editing is the shaping of the pot.

And when the pot is strong, people can drink from it without fear.

CHAPTER 2: THE SELF-EDITING MINDSET I HAD TO LEARN

When I began publishing seriously, I thought editing was mainly a skill. I believed that if I learned enough rules, bought enough tools, and watched enough tutorials, I would edit well. Later, I discovered something uncomfortable: editing is not only skill. It is character. It is patience. It is the ability to treat my own words like they belong to someone else.

Self-editing is one of the hardest tasks in the whole writing life because I am emotionally attached to what I wrote. My first draft carries my sweat. It carries my late nights. It carries my pride. Sometimes it carries my pain. That attachment makes me blind in ways I do not notice until a reader points it out.

So I had to learn a mindset before I could learn a method.

This chapter is about that mindset. It is about how I became the kind of writer who can revise without ego, cut without grief, and strengthen a book without destroying its heart.

Why I Cannot Edit Well Without Distance and Discipline

Distance Is Not a Luxury

The first time I tried to self-edit a full manuscript, I edited too soon. I finished writing and immediately began fixing sentences. At the time, it felt responsible. I told myself, "I am serious. I am improving." But what I was really doing was staying emotionally trapped inside the draft.

When I edit too soon, my brain is still living inside the story or argument. I remember what I intended, so my mind fills in missing steps without realizing it. I glide over unclear passages because I already know the meaning. I ignore holes because my memory

13

covers them. I read quickly because I am still excited by my own ideas.

That is not editing. That is admiration.

Distance is what turns admiration into evaluation.

Distance is a mental reset. It gives me the ability to read the manuscript the way a stranger reads it. It reduces attachment. It reduces the "I worked hard on this" emotion. It makes the book less sacred, which is necessary, because self-editing requires surgery, not worship.

Distance can be created in several ways:

- Time away from the draft
- Switching formats (screen to print)
- Changing font and layout
- Reading out loud
- Letting a trusted reader see it first
- Reading on a different device

But the simplest form of distance is time. I step away and do something else. Even a few days can reveal mistakes I could not see before. A few weeks can reveal structural problems I felt but ignored while drafting.

Distance is not procrastination. It is part of the process.

Discipline Is Not a Mood

Distance helps me see. Discipline helps me act.

Without discipline, editing becomes a series of emotional decisions. I edit when I feel like it. I skip what feels painful. I polish what feels easy. I chase tiny changes because they give me quick satisfaction. I avoid structural moves because they feel risky.

Discipline turns editing into a system. A system does not depend on mood. A system depends on a schedule and a method.

Discipline shows up as practical habits:

- I edit in passes, not randomly.
- I set a start time and an end time.
- I keep a checklist so I do not forget steps.
- I separate writing days from editing days when possible.
- I track decisions so I do not argue with myself repeatedly.

One of the most important disciplines I learned is this: **I do not negotiate with the manuscript.** I treat it like a project with standards. If something is unclear, it must be fixed. If something repeats, it must be tightened. If something breaks trust, it must be removed or repaired.

Distance gives me vision. Discipline gives me execution.

The Objectivity Problem: How I Stop "Reading What I Meant"

The biggest enemy of self-editing is not laziness. It is familiarity.

Familiarity creates illusion. When I know what I meant, my brain does not read the words. It reads the intention behind the words. That is why I can stare at a paragraph for ten minutes and still fail to notice that the subject changes halfway through. My mind is not reading. My mind is remembering.

This is the objectivity problem.

To self-edit, I must become a stranger to my own writing.

I Accept That My Brain Lies to Me

This is the first step. My brain is efficient. It wants speed. It wants pattern recognition. It is designed to fill gaps. That is helpful in daily life. But in editing, it becomes a problem.

If I accept that my brain lies to me, I stop trusting my first read. I stop trusting my silent reading. I start building strategies that expose the manuscript's real quality.

I Change the Way I Read

Silent reading is too smooth. My brain can skate over awkwardness. So I use different reading modes:

1) Read out loud
Reading out loud slows me down. It forces me to hear rhythm and clarity. When I stumble, the reader will stumble. When I run out of breath, my sentence is probably too long. When I feel embarrassed reading it out loud, something is off in tone.

2) Read on paper
Paper changes everything. The screen is where I wrote the draft. The screen triggers memory. Paper feels different. Paper makes errors stand out. I can also use a pen to mark issues quickly.

3) Change the format
If printing is not possible, I change font, spacing, and size. I also change background color if I can. The goal is to make the manuscript look unfamiliar.

4) Read in reverse for mechanics
For proofreading, I sometimes read sentence by sentence, from the end backward. This breaks narrative flow and helps me see surface errors.

I Ask the Reader's Questions, Not My Writer's Questions

The writer's question is: "What was I trying to say?"

The reader's question is: "What does this mean right now?"

A reader does not have access to my intention. A reader only has access to the words on the page.

So when I edit, I train myself to ask:

- Who is doing what, and is it obvious?
- What does this paragraph add that the last paragraph did not?
- Why should the reader care here?
- What is the takeaway from this section?
- Is the meaning carried by concrete details, or is it floating?

This shift changes everything. It turns editing from self-expression to communication.

I Use "Cold Tests" to Measure Clarity

A cold test is any method that exposes whether the writing stands alone without my memory.

Here are cold tests I use:

1) The one-sentence test
After reading a paragraph, I try to summarize it in one sentence. If I cannot, the paragraph is unclear or unfocused.

2) The highlight test
I highlight the key sentence in each paragraph. If a paragraph has no key sentence, it may be filler. If two paragraphs have the same key sentence, I may be repeating myself.

3) The question test

I ask, "What question is this section answering?" If there is no clear question, the section may not have a clear purpose.

4) The "new reader" test

I imagine a reader who knows nothing about my background. Would they understand my references? Would they follow the logic? Would they know why the example matters?

Objectivity is not a talent. It is a set of habits that make honesty possible.

Consistency Checks: Names, Timelines, POV, Tense, Tone

Consistency is where many indie books lose professionalism. It is not because the author is unintelligent. It is because consistency requires tracking. It requires attention. It requires a system.

When a reader sees inconsistency, the reader's trust drops. Even small inconsistencies create doubt.

Here are the consistency areas I learned to watch like a hawk.

1) Names and Spellings

In fiction, names are sacred. In nonfiction, key terms are sacred. In memoir, places and people are sacred.

Common problems include:

- A name spelled two ways (Nyakor vs Nyakorh, Malik vs Malek)
- A place name shifting (Juba town vs Juba City, the same place but used inconsistently)
- A title changing (Dr. vs Doctor, Pastor vs Rev.)
- A term changing for no reason (self-editing vs self editing vs selfediting)

These seem small until they multiply. The reader starts to feel that the book is unstable. The reader begins noticing errors everywhere.

So I track names and terms in one place. I decide the spelling and stick to it.

2) Timelines and Sequence

Timeline errors can destroy credibility. Even in nonfiction, timeline matters.

Common problems include:

- Events described out of order without transitions
- Time jumps without explanation
- Contradictions ("two years later" followed by a date that does not match)
- Ages and dates that do not align
- Seasons and weather that contradict the setting

In fiction and memoir, timeline mistakes are especially damaging because the reader is building a mental map. If the map breaks, the reader gets tired.

To solve this, I create a simple timeline document, even if it is rough. I list key events in order. I include dates if relevant, or at least relative markers (before, after, later that week, the next year).

3) Point of View

Point of view is not only a fiction concern. Nonfiction has point of view too. It is the perspective of the narrator.

Consistency problems include:

- Switching from "I" to "we" without reason
- Switching from direct teaching to detached academic tone

- Switching from confident voice to uncertain voice midstream
- Switching from personal memoir voice to promotional voice

In fiction, POV errors are obvious. In nonfiction, they are subtle, but they still weaken the book.

If I am writing in first-person singular, I must maintain that voice. The reader must feel the same person speaking throughout, not a different speaker every chapter.

4) Tense

Tense errors are easy to miss because my brain autocorrects them while reading. I might write in past tense, then slip into present tense, then return to past.

In nonfiction teaching, present tense is common because I am instructing. In memoir scenes, past tense often dominates. If I mix them carelessly, the book feels unstable.

So I decide the default tense for the book and enforce it. When I break tense, I do it intentionally, not accidentally.

5) Tone and Emotional Temperature

Tone is one of the hardest things to keep consistent. Tone is the emotional temperature of the book.

A consistent tone does not mean the book is flat. It means the tone changes with purpose.

Common tone problems include:

- Suddenly becoming sarcastic after being serious
- Suddenly becoming preachy after being conversational

- Suddenly becoming too formal after being warm
- Suddenly becoming aggressive in a gentle guide
- Overpromising or exaggerating after being honest

Tone inconsistency confuses the reader because they do not know how to interpret the narrator. The narrator starts to feel unreliable.

I solve this by writing a tone note for myself:

- Who am I speaking to?
- What kind of guide am I in this book?
- What emotions are allowed, and what emotions are dangerous?
- What is my default voice?

Then I edit with that tone note in mind.

The Editing Identity Shift I Had to Make

At some point I realized: if I want to publish professionally, I must become two people in one body.

- The writer creates.
- The editor judges.

The writer is generous with ideas. The editor is strict with standards.

When I mix these roles, I suffer. When I separate them, I work faster and produce better books.

This is why distance matters. Distance gives me the ability to switch roles.

When I open a draft too soon, I am still the writer. I protect everything. I defend everything. I feel pain when cutting anything. I argue with feedback.

When I open it later, I can become the editor. I can say, "This is not working." I can cut with calm. I can rewrite with purpose.

Self-editing is a form of leadership. It is me leading my manuscript into maturity.

Practice Section: I Build a One-Page Style Sheet for My Book

A style sheet is one of the most practical tools I have for self-editing. It prevents me from making the same decision twenty times. It prevents inconsistency. It saves time.

This is not a complicated document. It can be one page. It can be messy. What matters is that it exists.

Here is exactly how I build my one-page style sheet.

My One-Page Style Sheet Template

A) Book Identity

- **Book title (working):** _____
- **Genre/category:** _____
- **Ideal reader:** _____
- **Promise in one sentence:** _____
- **Tone keywords (3–5):** _____

This section reminds me who the book is for and how it should feel.

B) Voice and Point of View

- **POV:** First-person singular ("I")
- **Narration style:** (example: direct teacher voice, storytelling teacher voice, academic-lite voice)
- **Do I use contractions:** Yes / No
- **Do I address the reader as "you":** Yes / No

- **Do I use rhetorical questions often:** Yes / No

This section protects my voice consistency.

C) Tense Rules

- **Default tense for teaching sections:** Present / Past
- **Default tense for stories/examples:** Present / Past
- **Special rule for flashbacks:** _____

I keep it simple. The goal is to prevent accidental shifts.

D) Spelling, Capitalization, and Punctuation Choices

- **English variant:** US / UK
- **Oxford comma:** Yes / No
- **Numbers style:** (example: spell 1–9, numerals 10+)
- **Preferred spellings:** (example: e-book vs ebook, self-publishing vs self publishing)
- **Key punctuation habits to enforce:**
  _____

This section makes the manuscript look professional and unified.

E) Names, Places, and Key Terms

- **Names list:** (spellings locked)
  - _____
  - _____
  - _____
- **Place names list:** (spellings locked)
  - _____
  - _____
- **Key terms list:** (definitions consistent)
  - Term: _____ Definition: _____
  - Term: _____ Definition: _____

This is where I prevent small errors that destroy trust.

F) Formatting Rules

- **Chapter headings style:** _____
- **Subheadings style:** _____
- **Lists style:** bullets / numbers / both (and when)
- **Italic and bold rules:** (example: italics for book titles, bold for key terms)
- **Quotation style:** double / single
- **Scene breaks or section breaks:**
  _____

This section matters because formatting is part of reader comfort.

G) Content Boundaries

This is my favorite part because it protects focus.

- **Topics I will not drift into:** _____
- **Common tangents I must cut:**
  _____
- **Claims I must support or soften:**
  _____
- **Words or phrases I overuse (watch list):**
  _____

This section keeps the book tight.

How I Use the Style Sheet While Editing

1. I keep it open while I edit.
2. Whenever I make a decision, I record it.
3. When I notice a repeated mistake, I add it to the watch list.
4. Before final proof, I scan the manuscript specifically for the watch list items.

That is it.

A one-page style sheet turns self-editing into a managed process instead of a guessing game.

Closing Thought for Chapter 2

Self-editing is not only about catching errors. It is about becoming the kind of writer who can face their work honestly.

Distance protects me from emotional blindness. Discipline protects me from random editing. Objectivity protects the reader from confusion. Consistency protects trust.

When I learned this mindset, editing stopped feeling like humiliation. It began to feel like stewardship. I am taking care of the book. I am taking care of the reader. I am taking care of my name.

And once I began to edit with this mindset, my writing improved, not only my books. My drafts became cleaner because I could see my patterns. My confidence became stronger because I knew I had a method.

A writer writes.
A professional writer rewrites.

CHAPTER 3: THE EDITING LEVELS AND WHAT EACH ONE FIXES

When I was new to publishing, I treated editing like a single event. I thought I would "edit the book" the same way I might clean a room. I would start at page one and move forward, fixing whatever I saw. That approach felt productive because I was always changing something. But it produced messy results. I spent hours perfecting sentences in a chapter that later needed to be reorganized. I corrected commas in paragraphs that later got deleted. I polished sections that later moved to another place where the tone no longer fit.

Then I learned a truth that changed everything:

Editing is not one task. It is a stack of tasks, and each level solves a different type of problem.

When I understand the editing levels, I stop wasting time. I stop mixing goals. I stop fighting the manuscript. Instead, I work like a publisher. I work in the correct order, solving bigger problems first, then smaller problems later.

In this chapter, I explain the four major levels of editing and what each one fixes: developmental editing, line editing, copyediting, and proofreading. I also show you how I run one chapter through all four levels in the right order, without losing my voice.

Why the Order Matters

The order matters because editing is like building. If I change the foundation, the paint on the wall may crack. If I move walls, the furniture arrangement must change. If I redesign the kitchen, the plumbing moves too.

So I follow this logic:

- **Developmental editing** changes the shape of the book.
- **Line editing** improves how the book reads.
- **Copyediting** corrects the technical surface and enforces consistency.
- **Proofreading** catches what slips through after formatting.

Each level can reveal new issues. But the purpose is clear: I do not polish what I may later cut. I do not obsess over punctuation when the structure is still unstable.

This order is not a rigid religion. But as a working system, it saves time and improves quality.

Level 1: Developmental Editing

Developmental editing is the big-picture edit. It is about whether the book works as a whole.

If I think of my book as a journey, developmental editing answers: "Does this journey make sense, and does it deliver what it promised?"

Developmental editing focuses on:

- Structure
- Plot or argument
- Pacing
- Missing logic
- Weak sections
- Redundant sections
- Reader expectations and genre delivery

1) Structure: Does the Book Have a Strong Spine?

Structure is the backbone. In nonfiction, it is the logical sequence of ideas. In fiction, it is plot architecture. In memoir, it is narrative shape and thematic arc.

During developmental editing, I ask:

- Does each chapter have a clear purpose?
- Does the book flow in a sequence that feels natural?
- Do I introduce concepts before using them?
- Are there missing steps in the reader's path?
- Are there chapters that should be merged or split?

A common problem is that I write chapters in the order I discovered ideas, not in the order the reader needs them. Developmental editing is where I re-order.

Another common problem is "topic drift." I start the book as one thing and slowly become another thing. Developmental editing brings the book back to its identity.

2) Plot or Argument: Does It Hold Together?

In fiction, plot must hold. In nonfiction, argument must hold. In memoir, the thematic logic must hold.

If a plot has holes, the reader feels cheated. If an argument has holes, the reader feels unconvinced. If a memoir has holes, the reader feels manipulated or confused.

I check for:

- Motivations that make no sense
- Events that happen without cause
- Claims that appear without support
- Conclusions that do not follow from premises
- Missing definitions or missing examples

A strong book does not merely state ideas. It carries the reader through a reasoning path or a narrative path that feels earned.

3) Pacing: Does the Book Move at the Right Speed?

Pacing is not only about thrillers. Pacing exists in every genre.

In nonfiction, pacing is how quickly I move from concept to example, from explanation to application. If I take too long, the reader gets bored. If I move too fast, the reader gets lost.

In fiction, pacing is tension control. In memoir, pacing is emotional rhythm.

During developmental editing, I look for:

- Chapters that drag
- Sections that repeat what was already said
- Scenes that do not move plot or character
- Explanations that are too long without payoff
- Abrupt jumps that feel like missing pages

A simple pacing rule I use is: **Every chapter must justify its existence.** If it does not add something new or deepen something meaningful, it is a candidate for cutting or combining.

4) Missing Logic: What Did I Assume the Reader Knows?

Missing logic is one of the most common problems in first drafts. It happens because I know the subject too well. I jump over steps because they feel obvious to me.

A reader is not inside my head. The reader has limited patience for gaps.

So I ask:

- Did I define terms before using them?
- Did I explain why a step matters, not just what it is?
- Did I give examples for abstract points?

- Did I connect "because" statements properly?

When I find missing logic, I do not automatically add more words. Sometimes the fix is a better transition. Sometimes the fix is a tighter explanation. Sometimes the fix is removing a complicated concept that does not serve the reader.

Developmental editing is where I decide what belongs in the book and what belongs in a future book.

Developmental Editing Outcome

After developmental editing, my manuscript should be stable. The structure should make sense. The book should deliver on its promise. I should know that the main journey is solid.

Only then do I move into line-level work.

Level 2: Line Editing

Line editing is the reading experience edit. It is where the manuscript becomes enjoyable, clear, and strong sentence by sentence.

If developmental editing is architecture, line editing is carpentry and interior design. It is about how the reader moves through each page.

Line editing focuses on:

- Flow
- Voice
- Repetition
- Sentence strength
- Clarity at the paragraph level

1) Flow: Does the Writing Glide Smoothly?

Flow is how smoothly one sentence leads to the next. Flow is about rhythm, transitions, and coherence.

I check for:

- Jarring sentence order
- Paragraphs with no clear topic sentence
- Abrupt shifts without transition
- Too many short sentences in a row (choppy)
- Too many long sentences in a row (heavy)

Good flow does not mean fancy writing. It means writing that carries the reader without friction.

One technique I use is reading out loud. If I stumble, the flow is off. If I run out of breath, the sentence is too long. If I get bored, the paragraph is not moving.

2) Voice: Does It Sound Like Me (and Like the Book I Promised)?

Voice is not decoration. Voice is identity. It is the narrator's presence in the text.

Line editing protects voice by removing what weakens it:

- Unnecessary filler phrases
- Hesitation words that dilute authority
- Over-explaining
- Sudden shifts into a different persona
- Overuse of "big words" that sound unnatural

Voice should feel consistent across chapters. The reader should not feel like a different author took over halfway through.

If I want voice consistency, I enforce my style sheet rules: POV, tone, and boundary lines.

3) Repetition: Am I Saying the Same Thing in Different Clothing?

Repetition is a first-draft disease. It happens because I am thinking while writing. I circle an idea again and again from different angles, trying to understand it.

That process is useful for me, but it can be exhausting for the reader.

During line editing, I look for:

- Repeated sentences with slightly different wording
- Repeated examples
- Repeated introductions ("What I want to say is...")
- Repeated conclusions ("So in summary...")

I keep the strongest version and cut the rest. If repetition is necessary for teaching, I make it intentional. I signal it. I simplify it. I do not let it grow accidentally.

4) Sentence Strength: Are My Sentences Doing Real Work?

Sentence strength is about precision and energy.

Weak sentences often have:

- Unclear subjects
- Too many abstract nouns
- Passive constructions that hide responsibility
- Extra words that add no meaning
- Vague verbs (do, make, get)

Strong sentences have:

- Clear subjects
- Strong verbs
- Concrete nouns when possible
- Focused meaning
- Clean rhythm

Line editing is where I tighten. I remove fluff. I make the writing direct. I turn fog into clarity.

Line Editing Outcome

After line editing, my manuscript should read well. It should feel professional. It should sound consistent. It should be easier to read, not harder.

Now the book is strong in experience. Then I move to technical correctness.

Level 3: Copyediting

Copyediting is the technical correction level. It is where I fix grammar, usage, punctuation, and consistency. Copyediting also enforces the style sheet.

Copyediting focuses on:

- Grammar and sentence correctness
- Word usage and correctness
- Punctuation
- Spelling
- Capitalization
- Consistency in terms, names, numbers, and formatting
- House style decisions (US vs UK, Oxford comma, etc.)

Copyediting is where readers stop tripping over errors. It is where professionalism becomes visible.

1) Grammar: Correctness Without Killing Voice

Copyediting does not mean making every sentence sound formal. It means making every sentence correct enough to support clarity.

I fix:

- Subject-verb agreement errors
- Pronoun errors
- Fragment sentences that confuse meaning
- Run-on sentences
- Misplaced modifiers

But I also protect voice. Sometimes voice includes sentence fragments used intentionally for emphasis. Copyediting is not a machine process. It is human judgment.

2) Usage: The Right Word Matters

Usage errors can damage credibility. The reader may not consciously explain it, but they feel the mistake.

I check:

- Homophones (their/there/they're)
- Common confusions (affect/effect, then/than)
- Word choice errors that change meaning
- Repeated weak words

Copyediting is also where I reduce redundancy and correct small clarity problems that remain.

3) Punctuation: It Controls Meaning

Punctuation is not decoration. It controls meaning. A comma can change the way a sentence is understood. A misplaced apostrophe can signal carelessness.

I standardize punctuation choices according to my style sheet.

4) Consistency: The Silent Professionalism

Copyediting enforces consistency:

- Names spelled the same way every time
- Numbers formatted consistently
- Headings formatted consistently
- Italics used consistently
- Quotes formatted consistently

This is where the book starts to feel "smooth" at a technical level.

Copyediting Outcome

After copyediting, the manuscript should be clean and consistent. Most errors should be gone. The book should feel polished even before layout.

Then comes the final gate.

Level 4: Proofreading

Proofreading is the final surface check **after formatting.**

This is crucial. Formatting creates new errors. Page breaks, line breaks, hyphenation, missing words, repeated words, and spacing issues can appear during layout.

Proofreading focuses on:

- Typos and spelling errors
- Missing words
- Double words ("the the")
- Incorrect punctuation that slipped through
- Layout issues (widows/orphans, weird spacing)

- Incorrect page headers, page numbers, TOC errors
- Formatting consistency issues

Proofreading is not where I rewrite paragraphs. Proofreading is where I catch what is left before the book becomes permanent.

If I start rewriting during proofreading, I may introduce new errors and break formatting. So I keep proofreading strict.

Proofreading Outcome

After proofreading, the book should be ready for publication. This is the moment I can press publish with peace.

Practice Section: I Run One Chapter Through All Four Levels (In the Right Order)

Now I will show you exactly how I process one chapter, step by step. This is the part that turns theory into action.

To keep it practical, I treat "one chapter" as a unit. I do not edit the entire book at once. I work chapter by chapter after the developmental stage is completed for the whole manuscript.

Here is my method.

Step 1: Developmental Pass on the Chapter (20–40 minutes)

I ask four questions:

1. **What is this chapter's job?**
   I write one sentence: "This chapter helps the reader ___."
2. **Does the chapter deliver that job?**
   If not, I list what is missing.
3. **Is anything unnecessary?**
   I mark sections that repeat earlier content or do not move the reader forward.

4. **Is the order correct?**
   I check whether the chapter's sequence makes sense.

Then I do big moves:

- Cut entire sections if needed
- Move paragraphs or sections
- Add missing steps or missing examples
- Rewrite the opening if it does not set purpose
- Rewrite the closing if it does not land the takeaway

I do not care about perfect sentences yet. This is structural.

Step 2: Line Edit Pass (30–90 minutes)

Now I read the chapter out loud. I focus on the reader's experience.

I do the following:

- Tighten long sentences
- Fix unclear references
- Remove filler phrases
- Strengthen verbs
- Combine repetitive paragraphs
- Improve transitions
- Make sure the tone matches the rest of the book
- Make sure my "I" voice is consistent and natural

I also mark any repeated words and replace some of them, but I do not obsess. The goal is flow and strength.

Step 3: Copyedit Pass (30–60 minutes)

Now I switch into technical mode. I open my style sheet and enforce it.

I check:

- Spelling and capitalization
- Grammar issues
- Punctuation
- Consistency in terms and names
- Numbers and formatting rules
- Headings style and list formatting

I use tools if I have them, but I do not accept changes blindly. I remain the final judge.

Step 4: Proofread Pass After Formatting (20–45 minutes)

After the chapter is in the formatted layout (ebook or print proof), I proof it.

I check:

- Missing words
- Repeated words
- Spacing and indentation
- Page breaks and section breaks
- Heading consistency
- Table of contents links (for ebook)
- Header/footer issues (for print)

I mark corrections and apply them carefully. I keep changes small to avoid creating new problems.

My Final Sign-Off Questions

Before I call the chapter done, I ask:

- Does this chapter clearly serve its purpose?
- Does it read smoothly?
- Is it consistent with my book's voice and style?

- Is it clean enough that a reader will not be distracted?

If I can answer yes, I move to the next chapter.

Closing Thought for Chapter 3

When I understand the editing levels, editing becomes calm. It stops being a chaotic fight. It becomes a controlled process.

Developmental editing makes the book work.
Line editing makes the book read well.
Copyediting makes the book correct and consistent.
Proofreading makes the book publication-ready.

This is how I protect my reader. This is how I protect my name.
This is how I publish books that last.

CHAPTER 4: GENRES CHANGE THE EDIT (SO I EDIT FOR READER EXPECTATIONS)

If I had to name one mistake that quietly ruins many indie books, it would be this: the author edits the manuscript as if genre does not matter.

Genre always matters.

Genre is not just a label I choose on a publishing dashboard. Genre is the agreement I make with the reader before they read the first page. The cover signals genre. The title signals genre. The description signals genre. The first paragraph either confirms that agreement or breaks it.

That is why I do not touch the red pen until I know what kind of book I am editing and who it is for. Editing without genre clarity is like cooking without knowing who is coming to dinner. The meal may be delicious, but it may not be what the guest needs or expects.

This chapter is about editing as a reader-centered craft. It is about treating genre as a set of expectations I must either meet or intentionally subvert. It is about learning to edit with the reader in mind, not only with my own taste.

How I Identify My Genre and Audience Before I Touch the Red Pen

Before I edit, I do a simple diagnostic. I ask myself questions that force the book to declare what it is.

1) I Name the Primary Genre, Not a Pile of Genres

Many authors want to add five labels because they want five audiences. That is understandable, but it often creates a confused book.

So I choose one primary identity:

- Is this fiction?
- Is this nonfiction?
- Is this memoir?
- Is this academic or research-based work?

Then I get more specific.

Fiction: thriller, romance, fantasy, literary, sci-fi, mystery, historical.
Nonfiction: self-help, business, leadership, devotional, how-to, guide, essay collection.
Memoir: survival story, travel memoir, spiritual journey, family history, trauma-to-growth arc.
Academic: thesis-like argument, policy analysis, research synthesis, methodology-driven study.

If I cannot name the genre, the reader will not know either. If the reader cannot name it, they will not know how to read it. If they do not know how to read it, they will lose patience.

So I force myself to choose.

2) I Identify the Reader's Job

Different genres require different reader effort.

A thriller asks the reader to follow tension and clues.
A self-help guide asks the reader to apply steps.
A memoir asks the reader to trust a voice and enter a life.
An academic work asks the reader to engage evidence and logic.

I ask:

- What kind of attention does this book demand?
- How much background knowledge does it assume?
- How fast should it move?
- How emotionally intense should it be?

When I know the reader's job, I can edit to support it.

3) I Study Comparable Books (Not to Copy, but to Calibrate)

I do not need to imitate anyone. But I must understand market expectations.

So I study a few comparable books in my category. I observe:

- How the opening works
- How chapters are structured
- How long sections tend to be
- How much explanation is normal
- What tone is common
- How promises are made and fulfilled

This is not about losing voice. It is about learning the language of the genre so I can speak it clearly.

4) I Write a Clear Promise Before Editing

Before I edit, I write what I call an "ideal reader promise." It is a short statement that answers:

- Who is this for?
- What does it deliver?
- What experience will the reader have?

If I cannot write that promise, I cannot edit well. Editing is decision-making. Decisions need criteria. The promise becomes my criteria.

5) I Decide What I Refuse to Do

This is important. Editing becomes cleaner when I set boundaries.

If I am editing a self-help guide, I refuse to turn it into a memoir.
If I am editing a memoir, I refuse to turn it into a textbook.
If I am editing an academic work, I refuse to turn it into a motivational speech.

I can still include stories in nonfiction. I can still include feeling in academic work. I can still include ideas in memoir. But the core identity must remain stable.

Once I settle genre and reader expectations, editing becomes sharper. I do not cut randomly. I cut what violates the book's identity.

Editing Fiction vs Nonfiction vs Memoir vs Academic Work

Now I will break down how genre changes my edit. The goal is not to make you memorize rules. The goal is to help you understand what each genre demands from the editor.

1) Editing Fiction

Fiction lives and dies on immersion. The reader must forget they are reading words and start living in a world. That is the magic.

When I edit fiction, my main job is to protect that immersion.

What I Prioritize in Fiction Editing

Plot logic
Does cause lead to effect? Do decisions have consequences? Are there holes?

Character motivation
Do characters behave in a way that makes sense given who they are? If they change, is the change earned?

Pacing and tension
Is there forward movement? Does each scene add pressure, reveal something, or deepen stakes?

Scene purpose
Every scene must do at least one job: move plot, develop character, or build world in a way that matters. A beautiful scene that does none of these is a luxury I cannot always afford.

Dialogue realism and function
Dialogue should sound human, but it must also serve story. It must reveal conflict, desire, fear, or information. Dialogue that exists only to explain backstory becomes dull.

Point of view discipline
POV slips destroy immersion. A reader does not want to feel like the camera jumps inside random heads without warning.

What I Cut in Fiction

- Exposition dumps that slow the story
- Scenes that repeat the same emotional beat
- Over-explained motives (I let actions show)
- Repeated descriptions of the same setting
- Forced symbolism that feels like a lecture

What I Clarify in Fiction

- Who is speaking in dialogue
- Where the characters are in space during action
- Time and sequence of events
- Stakes, especially early on
- Character desires in a scene

The rule I keep in mind is simple: **fiction is felt before it is analyzed.** If the reader's feelings are not engaged, the book fails no matter how correct the grammar is.

2) Editing Nonfiction

Nonfiction lives on usefulness and clarity. The reader wants value. They want guidance, insight, instruction, or understanding.

When I edit nonfiction, my main job is to protect the reader's time and deliver the promise.

What I Prioritize in Nonfiction Editing

A clear thesis or central promise
What is this book teaching? What change does it create?

Logical sequence
Do the chapters build on one another? Does the reader have what they need before each step?

Examples and application
Abstract ideas must be grounded. If I teach a concept, I must show it in action.

Authority without arrogance
The voice must be confident, but not inflated. Readers can smell exaggeration.

Repetition management

Nonfiction often repeats because the author is teaching. That repetition must be controlled. I repeat strategically, not accidentally.

Action steps where appropriate

If the book is practical, the reader should be able to do something after reading.

What I Cut in Nonfiction

- Long personal tangents that do not serve the lesson
- Overly long definitions that delay action
- Overuse of filler phrases ("what I want to say is...")
- Claims that sound big but have no substance
- Marketing language inside the content

What I Clarify in Nonfiction

- Key terms and definitions
- Why a step matters, not just what it is
- Common mistakes readers make
- The difference between theory and practice
- The boundaries of my claims (what this does not solve)

Nonfiction editing is less about beauty and more about function. Beauty still matters, but function is the foundation.

3) Editing Memoir

Memoir is the most delicate edit because it carries personal truth and emotional weight. Memoir is not a diary. Memoir is crafted. But it must still feel honest.

When I edit memoir, my main job is to protect authenticity while building a strong narrative experience.

What I Prioritize in Memoir Editing

Truthful voice
The reader must feel the narrator is real. Not perfect. Real.

A thematic arc
Memoir is not just "things that happened." Memoir is "what it meant." The theme ties the story together.

Scene selection
Not every life event belongs in the book. The memoir editor's job is to choose scenes that serve the theme.

Emotional pacing
Too much intensity without rest exhausts readers. Too little intensity makes the memoir flat. I manage emotional rhythm like a musician.

Clarity of relationships
Readers must understand who people are and why they matter. Confusing family trees and unclear relationships weaken memoir.

What I Cut in Memoir

- Scenes that feel like revenge, not reflection
- Repetition of the same pain without new meaning
- Long explanations that interrupt scene momentum
- Moralizing lectures that feel disconnected from lived experience
- Unnecessary detail that belongs in private memory, not public storytelling

What I Clarify in Memoir

- Time markers (when did this happen?)
- Relationships (who is this person?)
- Place markers (where are we?)

- What the narrator knew then vs what the narrator knows now
- Why a scene matters to the theme

Memoir editing is about shaping truth into a story without betraying it. That balance is an art.

4) Editing Academic Work

Academic work has a different standard. It must be defensible. It must be structured. It must handle evidence carefully.

When I edit academic work, my main job is to protect credibility.

What I Prioritize in Academic Editing

A precise research question or thesis
If the question is fuzzy, the whole work becomes fuzzy.

Argument structure
Claims must be connected logically. The reader must see how evidence supports conclusions.

Evidence and citation discipline
Academic writing is judged by its proof. Unsupported claims can destroy credibility.

Terminology consistency
Key terms must be defined and used consistently. Shifting definitions is a fatal flaw.

Tone and formality control
Academic voice is not cold for no reason. It is disciplined because precision matters.

Methodology clarity
If research methods are used, they must be explained clearly. Even

in a literature-based work, the method of selection and analysis should be clear.

What I Cut in Academic Work

- Emotional language that weakens objectivity
- Sweeping generalizations without evidence
- Long personal stories that do not serve the research question
- Claims that feel like activism rather than analysis
- Repetition of definitions across chapters

What I Clarify in Academic Work

- Definitions at the point of first use
- The logic chain from evidence to conclusion
- Scope limitations
- Counterarguments and responses
- The difference between data and interpretation

Academic editing is strict because it has to be. Credibility is fragile in academic work. One careless claim can damage the whole piece.

Tone Discipline: What I Keep, What I Cut, What I Clarify

Tone is the emotional voice of the book. It is how the book feels while it teaches, tells, argues, or reflects.

Tone discipline is one of the most powerful editing tools I have. It prevents the book from sounding like multiple authors.

What I Keep

I keep tone elements that serve the book's identity:

- A consistent narrator presence
- A consistent level of formality

- Consistent humor style (if any)
- Consistent emotional openness (especially in memoir)
- Consistent authority level (especially in guides)

If the book is warm and conversational, I keep that warmth. If the book is formal and academic, I keep that discipline.

What I Cut

I cut tone elements that break trust or confuse expectations:

- Sudden preaching in a practical guide
- Sudden marketing language in the middle of a chapter
- Sudden anger that feels uncontrolled
- Jokes that do not fit the subject
- Long moral speeches in a scene-based memoir
- Sarcasm that makes the narrator feel unreliable

Tone breaks are not always wrong, but they must be intentional. If a break is accidental, I remove it.

What I Clarify

Tone often becomes unclear when the purpose is unclear.

So I clarify:

- Why a story is included in nonfiction
- Why a personal reflection belongs in a chapter
- What the reader should take away from an example
- When the narrator is speaking from the past vs the present
- What is fact vs opinion (especially in academic and nonfiction)

Tone discipline is not about being stiff. Tone discipline is about being stable.

Practice Section: I Write My "Ideal Reader Promise" in 5 Lines

This practice is one of the most useful editing tools I have because it forces the book to become honest.

I write the ideal reader promise before serious editing and I keep it visible while I work.

Here is how I do it, in five lines.

My 5-Line Ideal Reader Promise Template

Line 1: Who is this book for?
"I wrote this book for _____."

Line 2: What problem does the reader have?
"You are struggling with _____."

Line 3: What will this book help the reader do?
"By reading this, you will be able to _____."

Line 4: What kind of experience will the reader have?
"This book will feel _____."
(example: practical and direct, story-driven and honest, research-based and disciplined)

Line 5: What is the result if the reader applies it?
"When you finish, you will _____."

Example (Generic, For an Editing Guide Like This One)

1. I wrote this book for indie authors who want professional-quality manuscripts without guessing.
2. You are struggling with messy drafts, inconsistent voice, and uncertainty about what to fix first.

3. By reading this, you will be able to edit in levels, build a clear workflow, and prepare a book that earns trust.
4. This book will feel practical, honest, and step-by-step, with enough depth to make you confident.
5. When you finish, you will publish with peace because you know your book has been refined properly.

That is the promise.

Now, every time I make an editing decision, I ask: does this change support the promise or weaken it?

If it supports the promise, I keep it.
If it weakens the promise, I cut it.
If it confuses the promise, I clarify it.

Closing Thought for Chapter 4

Genre is not a box that limits me. Genre is a map that guides the reader. When I edit with genre in mind, I respect the reader's expectations and protect the book's identity.

Fiction needs immersion.
Nonfiction needs usefulness.
Memoir needs authenticity shaped into story.
Academic work needs credibility and precision.

When I stop editing as if all books are the same, my work improves immediately. My edits become sharper. My tone becomes stable. My readers become happier.

And the best part is this: editing for genre does not kill my voice. It strengthens it. It turns voice into a trustworthy guide that the reader wants to follow to the last page.

CHAPTER 5: MY SELF-EDITING WORKFLOW (THE PASS SYSTEM)

For a long time, editing felt like a swamp. I would open my draft and start "fixing." I would change a sentence, then change a paragraph, then doubt an entire chapter, then correct punctuation, then rewrite the opening, then wonder if the whole book was a mistake. I was working, but I was not progressing. I was editing in circles.

The breakthrough came when I stopped treating editing as one activity and started treating it as a sequence of passes. A pass system gave me boundaries. It told me what I am allowed to do today and what I am not allowed to do today. It forced me to stop polishing the wrong things at the wrong time.

A pass system makes editing predictable. Predictable editing becomes repeatable. Repeatable editing becomes a publishing pipeline.

This chapter is my pass system, the exact workflow I use to take a manuscript from raw draft to publication-ready book. It works for nonfiction, fiction, memoir, and most practical genres, with small adjustments. It is designed for indie authors who must manage time, money, and energy while still producing professional quality.

Why a Pass System Works

A pass system works because it separates problems.

If I try to solve structure, tone, clarity, grammar, and formatting all at once, my brain gets overwhelmed and my decisions become random. But if I dedicate a full pass to one category of problems, my mind becomes focused and my results improve.

A pass system also prevents a common trap: **polishing what I will later delete.** If I correct every comma before I confirm that the chapter belongs in the book, I waste time. If I rewrite sentences before confirming structure, I risk rewriting content that will move elsewhere.

So I edit from large to small:

- First, I make sure the book works.
- Then, I make sure it reads well.
- Then, I make sure it is correct.
- Then, I make sure it is clean after formatting.

That order protects my time and protects the reader.

Before I start, I do one important thing: I create or update my one-page style sheet. That style sheet becomes my law during the later passes. If I do not have it, I end up making decisions over and over again.

Now let me walk you through each pass.

Pass 1: Structure and Message (Big Moves Only)

Pass 1 is where I become ruthless and wise. This is not a grammar pass. This is not a sentence pass. This is the pass where I decide what the book actually is and whether it delivers its message.

The rule of Pass 1 is simple: **Big moves only.**

If I catch a typo, I ignore it. I can mark it if I want, but I do not fix it. Typos are noise at this stage. Structure is signal.

What I Do in Pass 1

1) I restate the book's promise.
Before I touch anything, I write one sentence that defines the book:

- "This book helps the reader ___."
- "This novel delivers ___ experience."
- "This memoir explores ___ theme through ___ journey."

If I cannot write this, the book is not ready for editing. It is still searching for itself.

2) I evaluate the table of contents or chapter list.
I look at the chapter titles and ask:

- Does the sequence make sense?
- Does it build logically?
- Are there missing steps?
- Are there repeated topics?

In fiction, I ask: does the plot rise? Do stakes increase? Is there a midpoint shift? Does the ending feel prepared?

3) I cut or relocate what does not serve the promise.
This is where many authors suffer. We want to keep everything because we worked hard on it. But editing is not about fairness to my labor. Editing is about service to the reader.

So I decide:

- What belongs in the book
- What belongs in an appendix
- What belongs in a future book
- What belongs nowhere

4) I strengthen the chapter purposes.

Every chapter must have a job. I write one sentence at the top of the chapter craft:

- "This chapter exists to ___."

If I cannot define that job, the chapter is in danger. It may need to be merged, split, or removed.

5) I fix missing logic and missing steps.

In nonfiction, this is crucial. I ask:

- Did I define key terms?
- Did I explain why a step matters?
- Did I assume knowledge the reader may not have?
- Did I jump from problem to solution too fast?

In fiction or memoir, I ask:

- Did I show why a character makes a decision?
- Did I explain enough of the setting for orientation?
- Did I create stakes that feel real?

6) I reshape openings and closings.

Pass 1 is where I repair structure at the macro level. That includes chapter openings and closings.

Openings must pull the reader in and set direction. Closings must land the point, build anticipation, or seal meaning.

What I Do Not Do in Pass 1

- I do not polish sentences.
- I do not correct punctuation.
- I do not worry about word choice.
- I do not rewrite for style.

Pass 1 is surgery, not makeup.

The Outcome of Pass 1

After Pass 1, the book should have a stable structure and a clear message. I should be able to explain the journey and the sequence. The draft will still be messy at the line level, but it will finally be the right book.

Pass 2: Scene/Section Purpose, Transitions, Redundancy

Pass 2 is where I strengthen the internal flow. The big structure exists now, but the book can still feel choppy. Chapters can still feel unfocused. Sections can still wander.

Pass 2 is about purpose and movement.

If Pass 1 answers, "Does the book work?" Pass 2 answers, "Does the book move?"

What I Do in Pass 2

1) I check every scene or section for purpose.
In nonfiction, I treat sections like "scenes" in terms of function. In fiction and memoir, I literally check scenes.

I ask:

- What is the purpose of this scene/section?
- Does it change something?
- Does it deliver new information, tension, insight, or development?

If a scene or section does not change anything, it is likely filler.

2) I strengthen transitions.

Many drafts suffer not because the ideas are weak, but because the connections between ideas are weak.

So I look for:

- Paragraphs that jump
- Sections that shift topic without warning
- Scenes that move location/time without orientation

Then I write transitions that guide the reader. A transition can be as simple as one sentence that signals movement:

- "Now that we have ___, we can look at ___."
- "The next morning, everything changed."
- "What I did not understand then was ___."

Transitions are small, but they carry the whole book.

3) I eliminate redundancy.

Redundancy is where the draft becomes heavy. It happens because I was thinking while writing. I explained an idea, then explained it again, then again with a different example.

In Pass 2, I hunt redundancy intentionally.

I look for:

- Two sections teaching the same lesson
- Two scenes delivering the same emotional beat
- Repeated definitions
- Repeated "setup" paragraphs

Then I decide: which is the strongest version? Keep that one. Cut the rest.

If repetition is necessary for teaching, I make it strategic. I simplify it and place it where it actually helps the reader, not where it helps my drafting process.

4) I manage pacing inside chapters.
Even if the book structure is solid, chapters can still drag. A chapter can spend too long setting up a point. A memoir scene can take too long before conflict arrives. A nonfiction chapter can explain too much before offering action.

So I tighten the internal pacing:

- Move the strongest point earlier
- Cut long warmups
- Replace long explanation with a sharper example
- Break long blocks into smaller movements

What I Do Not Do in Pass 2

- I still do not obsess over grammar.
- I still do not correct every typo.
- I still do not do detailed line-level polish.

Pass 2 is still structural, but at a smaller scale than Pass 1.

The Outcome of Pass 2

After Pass 2, the book should feel focused and smooth in movement. Chapters should feel purposeful. The reader should not feel lost or bored due to repetition.

Now the book is ready for sentence-level work.

Pass 3: Line-Level Tightening and Voice Consistency

Pass 3 is where the book starts to feel professional on the page. This is the pass where I improve the reading experience sentence by sentence, paragraph by paragraph.

I do not do Pass 3 until Pass 1 and Pass 2 are done, because Pass 3 is time-consuming. If I do it too early, I waste my time.

What I Do in Pass 3

1) I tighten sentences.
I remove unnecessary words. I simplify complex phrasing. I reduce clutter.

I look for:

- Vague verbs
- Abstract nouns without meaning
- Long sentences that carry two or three ideas
- Sentences with unclear subjects
- Weak openings like "There is" or "It is" that can be stronger

I do not try to sound fancy. I try to sound clear and direct.

2) I enforce voice consistency.
This is especially important in first-person books. The reader must feel the same narrator throughout.

I look for:

- Sudden shifts into formal language
- Sudden preaching tone
- Sudden academic tone in a conversational book
- Sudden slang that does not fit

If the voice shifts, I rewrite to bring it back.

3) I remove filler and throat-clearing.
First drafts often contain sentences that exist only because I was warming up:

- "What I want to say is…"
- "It is important to note that…"
- "In this chapter, we will…"

Sometimes these are useful, but often they are unnecessary. I cut them unless they truly help orientation.

4) I improve paragraph structure.
A strong paragraph usually has:

- A clear point
- Support (example, explanation, evidence)
- A closing that transitions or lands

If a paragraph has no point, it becomes fog. So I rewrite paragraphs so the main idea stands out.

5) I read out loud where it matters.
I do not read the whole book out loud unless I have time. But I do read key sections out loud:

- Opening chapters
- Closings
- Emotional peaks
- High-density teaching sections

The ear catches what the eye misses.

The Outcome of Pass 3

After Pass 3, the book should read smoothly. The voice should feel stable. The writing should feel intentional.

Now I move to technical correctness.

Pass 4: Mechanics and Style Sheet Enforcement

Pass 4 is copyediting mode. This is where I become strict. I bring my style sheet and enforce it across the manuscript.

If Pass 3 makes the book read well, Pass 4 makes the book look professional.

What I Do in Pass 4

1) Grammar and usage corrections.
I correct:

- Subject-verb agreement
- Pronoun errors
- Confused words
- Sentence fragments that harm meaning
- Run-ons

2) Punctuation consistency.
I enforce my punctuation decisions:

- Commas
- Quotation marks
- Apostrophes
- Dialogue punctuation (if fiction)
- Ellipses usage (and I keep it minimal)

3) Spelling and capitalization.
I lock spelling variations. I choose US or UK English and commit.

I standardize capitalization of key terms, headings, titles, and proper nouns.

4) Consistency sweeps.
I check:

- Names
- Place names
- Timelines (dates, ages)
- Terminology
- Numbers formatting
- Headings formatting
- Italics/bold rules

5) Style sheet updates.
Every time I make a choice that will repeat, I add it to my style sheet. This prevents future inconsistency.

Tools: Helpful, Not Final

I can use grammar tools here, but I do not accept changes blindly. Tools can miss context and can damage voice. I remain the editor.

The Outcome of Pass 4

After Pass 4, the manuscript should be mechanically clean and consistent. It is ready to be formatted.

Pass 5: Proof After Layout

Pass 5 is the final gate, and it must happen after formatting.

Layout creates new problems:

- Missing words at line breaks
- Spacing issues
- Widows and orphans in print

- Incorrect page numbers
- Broken table of contents links (ebook)
- Font inconsistencies
- Heading formatting errors

So I proof the formatted version, not the raw Word document.

What I Do in Pass 5

1) I proof slowly for surface errors.
I check:

- Typos
- Double words
- Missing punctuation
- Incorrect spacing
- Broken lines

2) I check layout consistency.
I scan:

- Chapter headings
- Subheadings
- Page breaks
- Indentation
- Lists
- Quotes

3) I verify front and back matter.
I check that:

- Table of contents is correct
- Page numbering starts correctly
- Front matter appears in the right order
- Back matter is consistent

4) I check ebook functionality.

If it is an ebook, I test:

- TOC links
- Chapter navigation
- Proper heading hierarchy
- Image sizing if any

5) I keep corrections minimal.

I do not rewrite paragraphs in Pass 5 unless something is clearly wrong. Big changes here can introduce new errors and break formatting.

The Outcome of Pass 5

After Pass 5, the book is ready to publish with confidence.

Practice Section: My Checklist for Each Pass

This is the practical core of the chapter. You can copy these checklists and use them as your editing system.

Pass 1 Checklist: Structure and Message

- I wrote the book's one-sentence promise.
- I confirmed the primary genre and reader expectations.
- I reviewed the table of contents or chapter list.
- I wrote a one-sentence purpose for every chapter.
- I cut chapters/sections that do not serve the promise.
- I reordered chapters for logical sequence or narrative rise.
- I identified missing steps, missing scenes, or missing logic.
- I strengthened chapter openings and closings at the big-picture level.
- I did not polish sentences or fix punctuation.

Pass 2 Checklist: Purpose, Transitions, Redundancy

- I checked every section/scene for a clear purpose.
- I removed scenes/sections that do not change anything.
- I strengthened transitions between sections and chapters.
- I eliminated repeated explanations and duplicated scenes.
- I tightened pacing inside chapters (cut slow warmups).
- I ensured each chapter builds forward momentum.
- I still avoided grammar perfection.

Pass 3 Checklist: Line-Level Tightening and Voice

- I tightened long sentences and removed clutter.
- I strengthened verbs and made subjects clear.
- I removed filler phrases and throat-clearing lines.
- I improved paragraph structure (point, support, landing).
- I checked voice consistency across chapters.
- I read key sections out loud.
- I ensured tone matches the book's promise.

Pass 4 Checklist: Mechanics and Style Sheet

- I corrected grammar, usage, and common confusions.
- I standardized punctuation based on my style sheet.
- I standardized spelling and capitalization (US/UK choice locked).
- I ran consistency checks for names, terms, numbers, and headings.
- I enforced formatting rules (italics, bold, quotes, lists).
- I updated my style sheet with decisions and watch list items.
- I confirmed the manuscript is ready for formatting.

Pass 5 Checklist: Proof After Layout

- I proofread the formatted file, not the raw draft.
- I checked for typos, double words, and missing words.
- I verified spacing, indentation, and page breaks.

- I checked chapter headings and subheading consistency.
- I verified table of contents accuracy and links (ebook).
- I reviewed front and back matter for order and correctness.
- I kept changes minimal to avoid introducing new errors.

Closing Thought for Chapter 5

A pass system gives me calm. It turns editing from fear into method. It stops me from drowning in details and helps me focus on the right problem at the right time.

Pass 1 makes the book true to its message.
Pass 2 makes the book move with purpose.
Pass 3 makes the book read with strength and voice.
Pass 4 makes the book clean and consistent.
Pass 5 makes the book ready for the world.

When I follow this system, I do not only produce better books. I become a better writer. Each pass teaches me what I keep doing wrong, so my next draft becomes stronger. Over time, my editing workload decreases because my craft improves.

That is the hidden gift of self-editing: it does not only save a book. It trains a career.

CHAPTER 6: WHEN I SHOULD HIRE AN EDITOR (AND HOW I CHOOSE ONE)

There is a moment every indie author reaches sooner or later. I sit with my manuscript, I have done my passes, I have tightened the sentences, I have corrected what I can see, and then a quiet fear rises: *What am I still missing?*

That fear is not always bad. Sometimes it is wisdom. Sometimes it is the signal that I have reached the edge of what I can do alone.

Indie publishing gives me freedom, but it also gives me full responsibility. If I publish an unedited book, the reader will not blame a publishing house. They will blame me. And if I publish a book that feels mechanically clean but structurally weak, the reader will still feel disappointed. In both cases, my reputation pays the price.

So I had to learn something important: hiring an editor is not an admission of weakness. Hiring an editor is a strategic decision about quality, time, and long-term trust.

This chapter is about that decision. It is about knowing when I should hire an editor, how I choose one wisely, and how I build a working relationship that improves the book without stealing my voice.

Signs I Should Not Go Alone

I do not hire an editor because it sounds professional. I hire an editor because it solves a real problem. Here are the signs that tell me I should not try to do it alone.

1) My Book Has High Stakes

If the book can create serious consequences when misunderstood, I should involve professionals.

High-stakes categories include:

- Medical and health content
- Legal guidance
- Financial advice
- Academic work that affects credibility
- Sensitive memoir that could harm people if handled carelessly
- Brand-building books that represent my public identity

Even if I know my subject, the book must be clear and safe for readers. An editor can help reduce risk.

2) I Keep Fixing the Same Chapter

If I return to the same chapter again and again, rewriting it without satisfaction, it means I am stuck. Stuck is expensive. Stuck is how books die.

In that case, an editor can do what I cannot do for myself: diagnose the real issue. Sometimes the issue is structure. Sometimes it is missing logic. Sometimes it is voice inconsistency. I might be polishing a problem that needs surgery.

3) Beta Readers Are Confused in the Same Places

If multiple readers highlight the same confusion, it is not a "reader problem." It is a manuscript problem.

When I see repeated feedback like:

- "I got lost here."

- "I'm not sure what the point is."
- "This section feels repetitive."
- "The pacing slows down in the middle."
- "I don't understand why the character did that."

That is a signal that the book needs more than surface cleanup. That is often developmental or line-level work. A professional editor can help.

4) I Cannot Tell What Level of Editing I Need

If I do not know whether I need developmental editing, line editing, copyediting, or proofreading, I am vulnerable. I can spend money in the wrong place.

A good editor can help me identify the correct level. If an editor tries to sell me the most expensive package without diagnosing what I need, that is a warning sign.

5) My Weaknesses Are Consistent Patterns

I have patterns. Every writer does.

Some authors repeat themselves. Some authors write unclear sentences. Some authors drift from topic. Some authors use too much passive voice. Some authors struggle with dialogue. Some authors struggle with transitions.

If I know my patterns, and I know those patterns are still visible in the manuscript, hiring an editor is not luxury. It is correction.

6) I Want to Publish Faster Without Losing Quality

Time is an invisible cost. If self-editing takes me three months but hiring an editor can shorten my process while improving quality, I should consider it.

This is especially true when I am building a catalog and publishing consistently. An editor can become part of my production system.

7) My Manuscript Is Long, Complex, or Multi-Threaded

The bigger the book, the more blind spots I have.

Long nonfiction guides, novels with multiple points of view, memoirs with complex timelines, and academic works with heavy citation demands all benefit from professional editing.

Complexity multiplies errors. An editor reduces them.

8) I Am Too Emotionally Close to the Material

Sometimes I can edit well technically, but the content is too personal. In memoir and autobiographical fiction, I may protect scenes because they matter to me, not because they matter to the reader.

If I cannot cut because I feel grief, I need help. A good editor can guide me toward shaping the story without disrespecting my experience.

What I Ask Before Hiring an Editor

Hiring an editor is like hiring a partner for a critical mission. I cannot choose purely by price. I cannot choose purely by friendliness. I cannot choose purely by a flashy portfolio.

I choose based on fit.

Here are the questions I ask before hiring. They protect my money and protect my book.

1) Genre Fit: Have You Edited Books Like Mine?

Genre fit is not optional. An editor who edits romance may not be the right editor for academic work. An editor who edits academic work may crush the voice of a memoir.

So I ask:

- What genres do you specialize in?
- What types of books do you edit most often?
- Can you show examples or references in my category?

I do not want an editor who says, "I can edit anything." That often means they have no deep expertise in reader expectations.

I want an editor who understands the rules of my genre, because they will protect reader trust.

2) What Level of Editing Are You Recommending and Why?

I ask the editor to diagnose what I need.

- Do you recommend developmental editing, line editing, copyediting, or proofreading?
- What problems in my sample suggest that level?
- What will you focus on in this stage?

If the editor cannot explain what they will do and why, they may not have a clear process.

3) Do You Offer a Sample Edit (and What Does It Include)?

A sample edit is where the truth lives. The sample shows me:

- How the editor thinks
- How they treat my voice
- How heavy their hand is

- Whether they clarify or rewrite
- Whether they explain their changes

I ask:

- How many words is your sample edit?
- Is it free or paid?
- What level of editing does it represent?

A good sample edit saves me from regret.

4) What Is Your Process?

I do not want an editor who works like a mystery.

So I ask:

- How do you deliver edits (tracked changes, comments, separate editorial letter)?
- Will I receive an editorial letter or summary notes?
- Do you edit in one pass or multiple passes?
- Do you offer a follow-up call or Q&A period?
- Do you want me to revise between rounds?

Process matters because editing is collaboration. If I do not understand the process, I will feel confused and frustrated.

5) Timelines: When Can You Start and When Will You Finish?

Deadlines matter, especially for indie authors managing releases.

I ask:

- When can you start?
- How long will the edit take?
- What factors might change the timeline?

- Do you offer rush services, and what do they cost?

I also ask about scheduling expectations:

- When do you need my manuscript?
- Do you require a deposit?
- What happens if I delay?

Clear timelines prevent conflict.

6) Boundaries: What Will You Not Do?

This is a surprisingly powerful question.

I ask:

- Will you rewrite in my voice, or will you suggest alternatives?
- Will you change my meaning, or will you ask questions when meaning is unclear?
- Will you flag sensitive content issues?
- Will you fact-check, or is that my job?
- Will you format, or is that separate?

Boundaries protect both of us. If I expect fact-checking but the editor does not do it, I will be disappointed. If the editor expects me to provide a style sheet but I do not, the project will suffer.

7) Communication: How Do We Work Together?

I ask:

- How do you prefer to communicate (email, shared doc, calls)?
- How quickly do you respond during the project?
- Do you allow questions during the edit or only after delivery?

The worst editing experiences come from unclear communication, not from grammar mistakes.

8) Pricing: What Am I Paying For, Exactly?

I do not only ask "how much." I ask "for what."

- Is pricing per word, per page, or per hour?
- What does the quote include?
- What does it not include?
- How many rounds are included?
- Is a revision review included?

If pricing is vague, I risk paying for less than I expected.

The Author-Editor Relationship: How I Protect My Voice While Accepting Correction

This relationship is where many authors either grow or break.

Some authors resist everything and learn nothing.
Some authors accept everything and lose their voice.

I refuse both extremes.

A good editor does not replace me. A good editor reveals me. They remove what hides my voice and strengthen what carries it.

Here is how I protect my voice while accepting correction.

1) I Decide What "Voice" Means in This Book

Voice is not just word choice. Voice is personality, rhythm, honesty, and worldview.

Before editing, I write a short voice note for myself:

- Who is speaking?
- What is the tone?
- How direct is the narrator?
- How personal is the narrator?

Then I share that with the editor.

If I do not define voice, I cannot protect it. I will only protect my ego.

2) I Accept That Being Edited Is Part of Being Published

If I publish, I invite judgment. Editing is simply judgment before the public gets it.

I remind myself: the editor's job is not to flatter me. The editor's job is to protect the reader.

When I accept this, feedback stops feeling like insult.

3) I Separate Three Types of Editor Comments

When I receive edits, I categorize them:

Type A: Objective corrections
Grammar, spelling, punctuation, factual inconsistencies. I accept these quickly unless they harm voice.

Type B: Clarity and structure issues
These are usually true. If the editor is confused, the reader will be confused. I treat these comments seriously.

Type C: Preference suggestions
This is the tricky part. Some changes are style preferences. An editor may prefer shorter sentences, or more formal tone, or less repetition. These suggestions can be useful, but they must align with my book's promise.

So I do not accept all Type C changes automatically. I evaluate them against my ideal reader promise.

4) I Keep Ownership of Meaning

An editor may suggest rewriting a sentence. Sometimes the suggested sentence is grammatically perfect but changes my meaning.

I watch for that carefully.

I accept edits that clarify meaning. I reject edits that shift meaning. I rewrite myself if needed, keeping meaning intact.

This is one of the most important principles:

The editor improves expression. I keep ownership of meaning.

5) I Create a Safe Method for Disagreements

Disagreements happen. They are normal.

When I disagree, I do not fight emotionally. I ask:

- What problem is the editor trying to solve?
- Is there a different way to solve it without losing my voice?
- Can I rewrite this section to satisfy both clarity and tone?

Often the editor's solution is not the only solution. If I can provide a better solution that fits my voice, that is my job.

A professional editor respects that.

6) I Choose an Editor Who Explains, Not Just Changes

I value editors who teach. Not every editor must teach, but I prefer it.

If an editor explains patterns:

- "You often bury the main point."
- "You shift tense during emotional scenes."
- "Your transitions are sometimes abrupt."

Those explanations help me improve long-term. They reduce my future editing costs because my drafts become stronger.

Practice Section: My "Editor Brief" Template (What I Send Before They Quote)

When I request a quote, I do not send only the manuscript and ask, "How much?" That creates vague quotes and misunderstanding.

Instead, I send an editor brief. This brief helps the editor understand my needs and reduces the chance of surprises.

Below is the exact template I use. You can copy it and fill it in.

Editor Brief Template

1) Project Title (Working):

---

2) Genre and Category:
Primary genre: _____
Secondary elements (if any): _____

3) Intended Audience:

Who this book is for: _____

Reader's main problem/desire:

_____

4) Ideal Reader Promise (One Sentence):

"This book will help the reader

_____."

5) Book Length and Format:

Current word count: _____

Target word count (if different):

_____

Formats: ebook / paperback / hardcover (choose)

Trim size (if known): _____

6) Editing Level Requested (If I Know):

Developmental / Line / Copyedit / Proofread

If I am unsure, I request: "Please advise what level is most appropriate and why."

7) What I Want You to Focus On:

Top priorities (choose up to 3):

- Structure and flow
- Clarity and readability
- Voice consistency
- Grammar and mechanics
- Consistency and style enforcement
- Pacing and engagement
  Other focus notes: _____

8) Voice and Tone Notes (Important):

Narrator voice: first-person singular ("I")

Tone keywords: _____

What I do not want: (example: overly academic tone, heavy rewriting, removing cultural flavor)

9) Any Sensitive Content or Special Considerations:
(example: trauma, cultural terms, real names, legal risk, faith content, etc.)

10) Style Preferences (If Any):
English variant: US / UK
Oxford comma: yes / no
Any special style rules: _____
Existing style sheet: yes / no (attach if yes)

11) Timeline:
When I can deliver the manuscript:

_____

My desired completion date (if any):

_____

Flexibility level: high / medium / low

12) Deliverables I Expect:
Please confirm what you provide:

- Tracked changes in Word or Google Docs
- Comments and queries in manuscript
- Editorial letter / summary notes
- Follow-up Q&A window (if offered)
- Second pass / revision review (if offered)

13) Sample Edit Request:
Do you offer a sample edit? yes / no
If yes: word count and cost: _____

14) Quote Request:
Please provide:

- Price structure (per word/page/hour)
- Total estimated cost
- Payment schedule (deposit + final)
- Estimated timeline
- Any additional fees (rush, extra rounds)

15) Contact Details:

Name: _____

Email: _____

Timezone: _____

Closing Thought for Chapter 6

Hiring an editor is not about proving I am serious. It is about protecting the reader and protecting my reputation.

I hire an editor when:

- the book is high-stakes,
- I am stuck,
- readers are confused,
- the manuscript is complex,
- or I want to move faster without losing quality.

I choose an editor by asking disciplined questions: genre fit, level of editing, sample edit, process, timelines, boundaries, communication, and pricing clarity.

And once I hire an editor, I remember this: the editor is not my enemy and not my boss. The editor is my partner in serving the reader. I protect my voice by defining it, and I accept correction by remembering why publishing exists in the first place.

A clean book is not luck. A clean book is a system. And sometimes, the system includes professional help.

CHAPTER 7: BUDGETING FOR EDITING WITHOUT DESTROYING MY PUBLISHING PLANS

If I am honest, money is one of the quiet reasons many indie authors either publish too early or stop publishing altogether. Editing costs can feel like a wall. I can write a book with only time and discipline, but editing, formatting, and covers often demand cash. When a writer sees quotes that feel high, two wrong reactions appear:

- I panic and publish without proper editing.
- I delay forever because I feel I cannot afford quality.

Both reactions damage the long-term publishing plan.

So I had to learn a better way: budgeting for editing like a publisher, not like a desperate writer. That means I treat editing as an investment with options, not as a punishment with one expensive path.

This chapter is about building an editing budget that protects quality without killing momentum. It is about understanding the cost drivers, choosing a realistic path, and creating a "quality budget" that matches my income level and publishing goals.

Why Editing Budgeting Matters More Than Most Authors Admit

Budgeting is not only financial. Budgeting is strategic.

If I spend everything on one book, I may not have funds to publish the next one. If I spend nothing on editing, I may publish books that destroy reader trust. Reader trust is harder to rebuild than money.

So my goal is balance:

- Publish consistently
- Maintain professional quality
- Avoid financial burnout
- Build long-term trust and catalog growth

A stable editing plan turns publishing into a system, not a gamble.

Typical Cost Drivers

Editing quotes are not random. They are driven by a few predictable factors. If I understand these factors, I can plan.

1) Manuscript Length

Length is the first cost driver. More words require more time. Editing is labor.

Editors may charge per word, per page, or per hour. No matter the method, word count affects cost.

This is why I always know my approximate word count before requesting quotes. If I send a manuscript without word count, I invite guesswork and confusion.

A practical lesson I learned: if my book is bloated, I pay more. That means tightening my manuscript before hiring an editor can reduce cost. Cutting unnecessary chapters is not only good for the reader. It is good for my budget.

2) Complexity

Complexity increases editing time.

Complexity can come from:

- Multiple POVs in fiction
- A dense cast of characters

- Complex timelines
- Heavy technical content
- Academic citations
- Specialized terminology
- Tables, charts, footnotes, and references
- A highly unique voice that must be preserved carefully

A straightforward 50,000-word romance novel is not the same editing job as a 50,000-word policy book with citations and definitions. Complexity affects cost.

If I know my manuscript is complex, I plan for higher editing investment or choose a hybrid approach.

3) Level of Edit

The level of edit is the biggest difference in price.

- Developmental editing is often more expensive because it requires analysis, restructuring guidance, and heavy feedback.
- Line editing takes time because it works sentence by sentence while preserving voice.
- Copyediting focuses on grammar, usage, punctuation, and consistency and can be faster than line editing, but still requires close attention.
- Proofreading is often the least expensive because it targets surface errors after layout.

A mistake many authors make is paying for the wrong level. If the manuscript has structural problems, paying for proofreading is like polishing a broken chair.

So I always diagnose what level I need before spending.

4) Manuscript Condition

An editor's quote is influenced by how clean the draft already is.

If my manuscript is:

- full of repeated sections,
- full of unclear sentences,
- inconsistent in tense,
- chaotic in structure,

the edit will take longer and cost more.

If I do my pass system first, I reduce the editor's burden, which can reduce cost or allow the editor to focus on deeper improvements.

This is why self-editing is not only about pride. It is about budget efficiency.

5) Turnaround Time

Speed costs money.

If I ask an editor to work faster than their normal schedule, I may pay a rush fee. Even if there is no rush fee, faster work can limit editor availability.

This is where planning saves money. If I schedule edits early and avoid emergency deadlines, I can often access better editors at better rates.

6) Editor Experience and Demand

Editors with strong track records and high demand often charge more. This does not automatically mean they are the best for me, but it does mean I must consider fit and budget.

Sometimes a mid-level editor with strong genre fit is better than a famous editor who does not understand my niche.

My rule is simple: **I pay for fit and outcomes, not for reputation alone.**

Three Paths I Can Choose

Once I understand cost drivers, I choose a path. There is no single correct path for every author. What matters is matching the path to my income level and publishing strategy.

Here are the three realistic paths.

Path 1: Full Professional Edit

This is the premium path. It usually involves hiring professional help for the main editing stages, often in sequence.

Depending on my needs, this could include:

- Developmental edit
- Line edit
- Copyedit
- Proofread

Sometimes one editor can do multiple stages, but often it is better to separate roles, especially for complex manuscripts.

When Full Professional Edit Makes Sense

- The book is a flagship brand builder
- The book will be heavily marketed and advertised
- The book is high-stakes (legal, health, financial)
- The book is intended to compete at a high level in a crowded market

- I am building a serious publishing brand and want consistent professional quality
- I lack the skill or time for thorough self-editing
- The manuscript is complex and needs experienced eyes

Pros

- Highest quality potential
- Strongest chance of excellent reviews
- Less risk of embarrassing errors
- Better long-term trust building
- Less stress if I have a strong editor team

Cons

- Most expensive path
- Requires cash flow planning
- Can slow publishing speed if I do not schedule well
- Risk of over-editing if the editor does not respect voice

How I Make Full Professional Editing Affordable

If I choose this path, I do two things:

1. I budget per project months ahead.
2. I reduce word count and clean the manuscript first so I do not pay for unnecessary work.

This path is not for every book. But for certain books, it can be worth it.

Path 2: Hybrid: Pro Editor Plus My Tool-Assisted Cleanup

The hybrid path is the most common path for serious indie authors who need quality but also need sustainability.

In this approach, I pay for professional help at the level that matters most, and I handle the rest with discipline and tools.

A typical hybrid strategy looks like this:

- I do Pass 1 and Pass 2 myself (structure and purpose)
- I hire a professional editor for line editing or copyediting
- I do a final tool-assisted cleanup and consistency sweep
- I hire a proofreader or do careful proof after layout

There are many versions of hybrid. The key is: I invest money where it makes the biggest difference.

When Hybrid Makes Sense

- I have decent self-editing skill but want professional polish
- I want consistent quality across many books
- I have limited budget but steady publishing plans
- I want to protect voice while still improving clarity and mechanics
- I am willing to do the work to reduce cost

Pros

- Strong quality at a lower cost than full professional editing
- Faster production if I manage my passes well
- I learn through the editor's feedback
- Sustainable for catalog building

Cons

- Requires discipline to do my share properly
- If I skip self-editing steps, I may waste the editor's time and money
- Tools can create false confidence if I rely on them too much

How I Use Tools Without Damaging Voice

Tools help me detect patterns, not replace judgment.

I use tools for:

- Spelling and basic grammar suggestions
- Repeated words
- Sentence length variation signals
- Consistency checks (names, capitalization)
- Passive voice detection

But I do not allow tools to rewrite my voice. I keep ownership of meaning and tone.

Hybrid editing teaches me to be both author and production manager.

Path 3: DIY Plus Beta Readers and Structured Passes

The DIY path is the most budget-friendly, but it requires the strongest discipline.

This path is not "no editing." This path is "I build my own quality system with careful passes and trusted readers."

A strong DIY approach usually includes:

- A full pass system (structure, purpose, line tightening, mechanics, proof after layout)
- Beta readers who match the target audience
- A style sheet for consistency
- Read-aloud checks
- Print proof or format proof checks
- Possibly a small paid proofread if budget allows

When DIY Makes Sense

- I am just starting and cash is limited
- I am writing shorter books or low-risk content
- I am publishing frequently and need sustainability
- I am building skill intentionally over time
- I have access to strong beta readers or critique partners

Pros

- Lowest cost
- Builds long-term skill
- Increases my independence as an author
- Makes publishing possible even with low income

Cons

- Highest risk of missing errors
- Can be slower if I do not have a strong system
- Requires emotional strength to accept reader feedback
- Can harm reputation if the DIY process is sloppy

How I Make DIY Professional

If I choose DIY, I become strict about process. I do not allow myself to publish without:

- Pass 1 and Pass 2 structural checks
- Pass 3 line tightening
- Pass 4 mechanics enforcement
- Pass 5 proof after layout

I also make sure beta readers are not just friends who say "nice." I need readers who will tell me where they were confused and where they got bored.

DIY can produce excellent books when the system is strong. But DIY cannot be lazy.

Choosing the Right Path Without Self-Deception

Many authors choose a path based on ego or fear, not on reality.

Ego says: "I do not need editors."
Fear says: "I cannot publish until it is perfect."

Both attitudes are dangerous.

I choose based on:

- the purpose of the book,
- the risk level,
- my current skill,
- my budget,
- and my publishing schedule.

A short practical guide for a small niche may do well with hybrid editing. A flagship book meant to represent my brand to the world may deserve full professional editing. A low-risk short book used to build catalog may be DIY with strong beta readers.

The book's role in my business determines the editing budget.

Practice Section: I Create a "Quality Budget" That Matches My Income Level

Now I will show you how I create a quality budget that is realistic. A quality budget is not a dream list. It is a plan I can execute.

The goal is to protect my publishing system while staying financially stable.

Step 1: I Define My Publishing Goal for the Next 12 Months

I start by writing:

- How many books I plan to publish this year
- Which book is the flagship
- Which books are catalog builders

Example:

- 1 flagship book
- 3 mid-level books
- 6 short catalog books

This matters because editing budget must match volume.

If I plan to publish 10 books but budget as if I will fully professionally edit all 10, I may collapse financially. A tiered plan makes more sense.

Step 2: I Assign Quality Tiers

I assign each planned book a quality tier:

Tier A: Flagship quality
This book represents my brand strongly. Highest editing investment.

Tier B: Strong professional quality
This book is important but not the flagship. Hybrid editing is often ideal.

Tier C: Solid baseline quality
This book is shorter or lower risk. DIY plus beta readers and strict passes.

This is not about lowering standards. Tier C still requires clean work. The difference is how much professional labor I pay for.

Step 3: I Estimate My Available Monthly Publishing Budget

I calculate what I can realistically invest each month without stress.

I write:

- Monthly income
- Fixed costs (rent, food, transport)
- Savings goals
- Remaining flexible amount

Then I choose a publishing allocation.

Example:

- 10% of my income goes to publishing expenses
  or
- A fixed amount per month goes to publishing expenses

The method does not matter. Consistency matters.

Step 4: I Create a "Publishing Quality Fund"

Instead of trying to pay editing costs suddenly, I build a fund.

Every month, money goes into this fund. It becomes my editing budget, cover budget, formatting budget, and marketing test budget.

This prevents panic spending.

Step 5: I Match Each Book Tier to a Real Editing Plan

Now I create the plan.

Tier A Plan (Flagship)

- Professional developmental or line edit (depending on need)
- Professional copyedit
- Proof after layout (professional if budget allows)
- My own passes before and after

Tier B Plan (Hybrid)

- My Pass 1 and Pass 2
- Professional line or copyedit
- My tool-assisted cleanup
- Proof after layout (DIY or paid based on remaining funds)

Tier C Plan (DIY)

- Full pass system
- Strong beta readers
- Style sheet enforcement
- Print proof check
- Optional small paid proofread if affordable

I write this plan for each book so I am not guessing later.

Step 6: I Set "Minimum Quality Non-Negotiables"

No matter the tier, I set minimum standards.

My non-negotiables include:

- A clear promise and stable structure
- Consistent voice and tone
- Clean mechanics (no obvious grammar issues)
- Proof after layout (even if DIY)
- Style sheet enforced for names and terminology

This protects reader trust even when budgets are tight.

Step 7: I Review After Every Release

After publishing, I do a quality review:

- What errors slipped through?
- What reader feedback appeared?
- What part of the process failed?
- What should I improve for the next book?

This review improves my system and reduces future editing costs because I become more skilled.

A Simple "Quality Budget" Worksheet

Here is a practical worksheet you can copy.

Monthly income: _____
Monthly fixed costs: _____
Monthly savings goal: _____
Monthly available for publishing: _____

Publishing Quality Fund target (monthly):
_____

Books planned this year: _____

Tier A books (flagship): _____
Tier B books: _____
Tier C books: _____

Tier A editing plan: _____
Tier B editing plan: _____
Tier C editing plan: _____

Minimum quality non-negotiables: _____

This worksheet turns editing from fear into planning.

Closing Thought for Chapter 7

Editing is not free, even when I do it myself. It costs time, attention, and energy. Professional editing costs money. The question is not whether editing costs. The question is whether I will pay the cost wisely.

When I understand cost drivers, I stop being surprised by quotes. When I choose an editing path intentionally, I stop feeling trapped. And when I build a quality budget that matches my income, I stop burning out.

Indie publishing is a long game. The winners are not the authors who spend the most or spend the least. The winners are the authors who build a system that keeps quality high and momentum steady.

A clean catalog is built book by book, decision by decision, and budget by budget.

CHAPTER 8: TECHNOLOGY THAT HELPS ME EDIT FASTER (WITHOUT REPLACING JUDGMENT)

When technology entered the writing world in a serious way, many indie authors reacted in one of two extremes.

One extreme is fear: "Tools will ruin my voice. Tools will make my writing sound fake. Tools will turn me into a machine."
The other extreme is blind trust: "Tools will fix my book. Tools will catch everything. Tools will make my writing perfect."

I had to learn a third way: tools are servants, not masters.

Technology can speed up my editing process and reveal patterns I would otherwise miss. But technology cannot replace my judgment. It cannot replace my intent. It cannot replace the cultural tone of my voice. It cannot decide what I mean.

So this chapter is about using technology with discipline. It is about extracting the benefits of tools without surrendering authority over my book.

If I use tools the right way, I edit faster and publish cleaner. If I use tools the wrong way, I publish a book that sounds like a stranger wrote it.

What Tools Are Good At

Tools do not "understand" my book the way a human does. But they are excellent at detecting patterns and surface-level issues. They are tireless. They do not get bored. They do not miss the same mistake twenty times because their mind wandered.

Here is what tools are truly good at.

1) Pattern Detection

Tools see repetition in a way that is hard for my human brain to see, especially across a long manuscript.

They can help me catch:

- Overused words and phrases
- Repeated sentence structures
- Repeated openings ("I want to...", "It is...", "There is...")
- Repeated transitions ("In conclusion...", "However...", "Therefore...")
- Repeated filler phrases ("In other words...", "What this means is...")

When I write a long book, I often develop verbal habits without noticing. Tools reveal those habits quickly.

Pattern detection is useful because it shows me where my writing becomes lazy or predictable. Then I can tighten the work intentionally.

2) Basic Grammar and Mechanics Signals

Tools are good at pointing out common issues such as:

- Subject-verb agreement problems
- Missing articles (a, an, the)
- Some punctuation errors
- Spelling mistakes
- Common confusions (their/there/they're)
- Extra spaces, doubled words, repeated punctuation

Tools do not catch every grammar issue, and they sometimes flag things that are not wrong. But as a first sweep, they reduce noise.

This is especially helpful before I send a manuscript to a human editor. The cleaner the draft, the more the editor can focus on meaningful improvements instead of obvious mistakes.

3) Repetition and Redundancy Clues

Tools can highlight:

- Repeated words in close proximity
- Repeated phrases across paragraphs
- Similar sentences that could be merged
- Overuse of intensifiers (very, really, extremely)
- Weak verbs and adverbs that could be strengthened

I do not let a tool decide whether repetition is bad. Sometimes repetition is a teaching strategy. Sometimes it is a literary choice. But tools reveal where repetition happens so I can decide whether it is intentional.

4) Readability and Sentence Length Awareness

Some tools provide readability scores and sentence length flags. These are not perfect measures, but they can warn me when a section becomes too heavy.

If a paragraph contains five very long sentences, the reader may feel tired. Tools help me notice that and vary rhythm.

I do not worship readability scores, but I do respect the warnings when they align with what my ear hears.

5) Consistency Assistance

Tools can help with consistency tasks such as:

- Standardizing capitalization
- Checking spelling consistency for names and terms

- Finding every instance of a word or phrase
- Locating inconsistent formatting patterns

For example, if I have two spellings of a character's name, a search tool or consistency checker can find every instance quickly. That saves hours.

Consistency work is where tools shine.

6) Workflow Speed and Organization

Technology helps me manage editing projects:

- Track changes
- Comments and version history
- Style sheets and templates
- Checklists and progress tracking
- Collaboration with editors and beta readers

Even simple features like "find and replace," "navigation pane," and "comment threads" reduce editing time dramatically.

The biggest speed improvement is not fancy AI. It is often basic document control and structure management.

What Tools Cannot Do

If I remember only one truth about editing tools, it is this:

Tools can correct form, but they cannot own meaning.

Here is what tools cannot do, no matter how smart they appear.

1) Tools Cannot Know My Intent

Intent is the engine of writing. Intent is what I am trying to achieve with a sentence, a paragraph, or a chapter.

A tool may suggest changes that make a sentence "cleaner" but change what I intended.

For example:

- A tool might remove a word that carries emotional nuance.
- A tool might replace a culturally grounded phrase with a generic alternative.
- A tool might change a sentence structure that is intentionally rhythmic.

If I accept those changes blindly, I lose my intended meaning.

So I treat tool suggestions as proposals, not as commands.

2) Tools Cannot Understand Voice

Voice is identity.

Voice includes:

- rhythm,
- cultural flavor,
- humor style,
- moral stance,
- storytelling habit,
- and the unique way I talk to the reader.

Tools often push writing toward a bland middle, toward what is "standard." That is dangerous for an author.

If I let tools standardize my voice, my book becomes technically correct but spiritually empty. It sounds like a corporate manual, not a human narrator.

This is especially dangerous in memoir and personal nonfiction, where voice is the reason readers stay.

3) Tools Cannot Handle Cultural Tone Reliably

If my writing contains:

- South Sudanese cultural references,
- indigenous terms,
- spiritual language,
- local metaphors,
- multilingual phrases,

tools may misread them. Tools may label them as errors. Tools may suggest replacements that remove meaning.

Cultural tone is delicate. A tool cannot carry it the way I can.

So I protect cultural tone. I do not let tools erase it.

Instead, I clarify for the reader when needed, but I keep the cultural truth intact.

4) Tools Cannot Decide What to Cut or Keep

Tools can highlight repetition, but they cannot decide which repetition serves teaching and which repetition is filler.

Tools can flag "wordiness," but they cannot judge whether a certain slow moment is needed for emotional weight.

Tools can suggest removing "redundancy," but they cannot judge whether a paragraph is building toward a payoff.

Cutting and keeping is editorial judgment. That is human work.

5) Tools Cannot Replace Ethical Responsibility

In nonfiction, especially in advice genres, there is ethical responsibility. What I claim matters. What I recommend matters. How I frame things matters.

Tools cannot guarantee that my book is fair, accurate, safe, or responsible. Only I can do that.

A tool may make a sentence sound more confident than it should. That can become dangerous.

I must keep control of truth and humility.

My Safe Tool Workflow: Suggestions, Not Automatic Rewriting

Because tools have strengths and weaknesses, I built a safe workflow. This workflow allows tools to assist me without hijacking my book.

The core rule is:

I do not allow tools to rewrite my manuscript automatically.

I only accept suggestions deliberately, one by one, with my judgment in charge.

Here is my workflow.

Step 1: I Finish My Pass System First (At Least Pass 1 and Pass 2)

I do not run heavy tool checks while my structure is still unstable. If I do, I waste time fixing sentences that may be moved or cut later.

So I wait until:

- Pass 1 (structure) is done
- Pass 2 (purpose and flow) is done

Then I use tools to support Pass 3 and Pass 4.

Step 2: I Create a "Tool-Safe Copy" of My Manuscript

Before running tools, I duplicate the file. I label the copy clearly.

This protects me from accidental bulk changes. It also allows me to compare versions if needed.

If I am working in a system with version history, I still create a clear checkpoint. Editing is safer when I can roll back.

Step 3: I Run Tools in Categories, Not All at Once

Many tools throw hundreds of suggestions at me. If I try to address everything at once, I get overwhelmed and start accepting changes blindly.

So I run tools by category:

- Spelling and obvious typos first
- Grammar suggestions next
- Repetition detection next
- Consistency checks next
- Readability flags last

This keeps my mind clear.

Step 4: I Apply Changes With a Rule of Meaning

My rule is simple:

- If a suggestion improves clarity without changing meaning, I accept it.
- If it changes meaning, I reject it or rewrite manually.
- If it threatens voice, I reject it or find my own alternative.

This rule protects my identity as an author.

Step 5: I Maintain a "Reject List" for My Voice

Tools often flag the same things repeatedly, including style choices that are intentional.

So I keep a reject list:

- words and phrases the tool keeps trying to "fix" that are actually my style,
- cultural terms,
- proper names,
- intentional sentence fragments,
- intentional rhetorical choices.

This reject list becomes part of my style sheet.

It saves time and prevents me from fighting the same battle repeatedly.

Step 6: I Save Tool Work for the Right Stage

I use tools most heavily during:

- Pass 3 (line tightening): for repetition and sentence strength clues
- Pass 4 (mechanics): for grammar, punctuation, consistency signals

Then I stop.

During Pass 5 (proof after layout), I do not rely on tools. I rely on slow human reading because layout issues are visual and contextual.

Step 7: I Do a Human Read After Tool Changes

This is crucial.

After applying tool suggestions, I always do a human read of the affected sections. Tools can create awkward rhythm. Tools can break flow.

So I read, out loud if possible, the paragraphs where I accepted many changes. If it sounds unnatural, I rewrite in my voice.

Tools do not get the last word. I do.

Practice Section: I Run a Tool Audit and Decide What to Accept and Reject

Now I will show you a practical exercise that makes tool use safer and more effective.

A tool audit is where I test how a tool behaves on my writing and decide how much I trust it.

This audit prevents me from letting a tool shape my voice unconsciously.

Step 1: I Choose a Sample Section (1,000–2,000 words)

I choose a section that represents the book's voice:

- not the most polished part,
- not the worst part,
- but a typical chapter section.

If the book has different modes (story + teaching), I choose a section from each mode.

Step 2: I Run the Tool and Collect Suggestions

I run the tool and do not accept anything yet. I just collect.

I note the categories:

- Spelling
- Grammar
- Wordiness
- Tone and style
- Repetition
- Clarity suggestions

Step 3: I Sort Suggestions Into Four Buckets

This is the heart of the audit.

Bucket A: Accept Almost Always

These are usually safe.

Examples:

- obvious typos
- double words
- missing punctuation that changes clarity
- basic grammar errors that are truly wrong

Bucket B: Accept Sometimes (Check Meaning First)

These require judgment.

Examples:

- sentence tightening suggestions
- rephrasing suggestions
- "wordiness" suggestions
- synonym suggestions

I only accept these if meaning and voice remain intact.

Bucket C: Reject Almost Always

These are harmful to voice or meaning.

Examples:

- suggestions that remove cultural tone
- suggestions that flatten my personal voice
- suggestions that change my moral stance
- suggestions that force unnatural formal tone

Bucket D: Needs Manual Rewrite

Sometimes the tool identifies a real problem but suggests a bad fix.

This bucket is valuable because it points to issues I should fix myself.

Examples:

- unclear sentences where the tool's rewrite is awkward
- paragraphs with weak flow
- repeated phrases that need a rewrite rather than a replacement

Step 4: I Calculate My Tool Trust Rate

I do not need math, but I do need a sense of accuracy.

I ask:

- Out of 20 suggestions, how many were helpful?
- How many were harmful?
- What types were most reliable?

If a tool is wrong half the time, I limit its use to spelling and basic mechanics. If a tool is helpful most of the time, I can use it more confidently.

Step 5: I Write My "Tool Rules" for This Book

Now I convert the audit into rules.

Examples:

- "I will accept spelling and obvious grammar corrections quickly."
- "I will reject tone changes automatically."
- "I will not accept synonym swaps unless I confirm cultural meaning."
- "I will treat 'wordiness' flags as prompts for manual tightening, not automatic cuts."
- "I will add all names and key terms to the tool's dictionary."

These rules become part of my style sheet and editing workflow.

Step 6: I Apply Tools to the Full Manuscript With Discipline

Now I run the tool on the full manuscript, but I apply changes according to my rules.

This prevents fatigue-based acceptance. Fatigue is the biggest risk when using tools. After 200 suggestions, I might start clicking "accept" just to finish. That is how voice dies.

So I edit in sessions:

- 45 minutes of tool review

- short break
- then return

I protect my judgment by protecting my energy.

Closing Thought for Chapter 8

Technology is powerful, but it is not wise. Wisdom belongs to the author.

Tools are excellent at detecting patterns, catching basic errors, and speeding up consistency work. They can help me edit faster, especially in Pass 3 and Pass 4. But tools cannot carry intent, meaning, voice, or cultural tone. If I forget that, I risk publishing a book that is clean but hollow.

My safe workflow keeps tools in their proper place:

- suggestions, not commands,
- assistance, not replacement,
- speed, not surrender.

When I use tools with discipline, I publish better books faster. When I use tools without judgment, I publish books that do not sound like me.

In indie publishing, my voice is my brand. My judgment is my authority. Tools can help me serve the reader, but they will never be the editor of record.

That editor is me.

CHAPTER 9: COLLABORATION AND FEEDBACK THAT ACTUALLY IMPROVES THE BOOK

For a long time, I believed feedback was simple. I thought I would give my manuscript to someone, they would tell me what they think, and I would magically know how to fix the book.

That is not how it works.

Most feedback is either too vague to use or too personal to trust. People say, "It's good," and I learn nothing. Or they say, "I don't like this," and I am not sure whether the problem is the book or the person.

So I had to learn a skill that matters as much as writing itself: how to collaborate and collect feedback that actually improves the book.

In indie publishing, collaboration is not a luxury. It is a quality strategy. No matter how skilled I am, I cannot fully see my own blind spots. I cannot read my own writing like a new reader reads it. I cannot reliably detect every confusion point because my brain remembers what I intended.

Feedback is how I replace intention with reality.

But to get real feedback, I must use the right people and ask the right questions. That is what this chapter is about.

Beta Readers vs Critique Partners vs Sensitivity Readers

Many authors lump all feedback into one category, as if every reader does the same job. That creates confusion and disappointment.

Different collaborators provide different kinds of value. If I use the wrong kind of reader for the wrong purpose, the feedback becomes noisy.

So I separate three roles clearly: beta readers, critique partners, and sensitivity readers. I do not treat them as substitutes. I treat them as tools in my editing system.

1) Beta Readers: "Does This Work for a Normal Reader?"

Beta readers are not editors. Beta readers are test readers.

Their job is to represent the target audience and answer one main question:

Does this book deliver the experience it promises?

Beta readers help me catch:

- Confusing sections
- Boring sections
- Pacing problems
- Emotional moments that do not land
- Unclear character motivations (fiction)
- Missing steps or missing examples (nonfiction)
- Places where the reader loses trust
- Chapters that feel repetitive

Beta readers are especially useful after Pass 1 and Pass 2, when the structure is stable enough to test.

What Beta Readers Are Not Good At

Most beta readers are not good at:

- Grammar correction
- Copyediting consistency

- Deep structural redesign suggestions
- Fixing sentence-level issues

They might notice a few typos, but if I rely on beta readers for technical cleanup, I will miss many errors.

Beta readers are about experience, not mechanics.

Who Makes a Good Beta Reader

A good beta reader:

- matches my target audience
- reads my genre willingly
- is honest
- can explain confusion clearly
- can finish the book
- does not try to rewrite it in their style

I do not need 20 beta readers. I need a few reliable ones who will actually read and respond.

2) Critique Partners: "How Can This Be Better at the Craft Level?"

Critique partners are different. They are often writers themselves or advanced readers with strong analytical ability.

Their job is to engage the craft:

- structure,
- voice,
- pacing,
- clarity,
- argument strength,
- and storytelling technique.

A critique partner can help me with deeper questions:

- Is this chapter doing what it should do?
- Is the argument convincing?
- Does the narrator's voice remain stable?
- Are my scene choices effective?
- Are my stakes strong enough?
- Are my transitions clean?

Critique partners are valuable earlier than beta readers, because they can help shape the manuscript before it becomes "final."

The Risk With Critique Partners

Critique partners can also become dangerous if I choose the wrong person. Some critique partners:

- turn every conversation into competition
- try to impose their voice on my writing
- focus too much on tiny issues and ignore big issues
- criticize without offering usable direction

A good critique partner points to problems clearly and explains why they matter. They do not attempt to become the author.

How I Use Critique Partners

I use critique partners for:

- a chapter or two at a time
- early developmental feedback
- problem sections where I feel stuck
- voice consistency checks

I do not need them to read the whole book unless they want to and have time. Sometimes one strong critique on a critical chapter saves me weeks.

3) Sensitivity Readers: "Is This Fair, Accurate, and Safe?"

Sensitivity readers serve a different purpose. They are not just reading for enjoyment. They are reading for representation, fairness, and harm prevention.

Sensitivity readers help when a book contains:

- portrayals of cultures, ethnicities, or communities
- faith traditions and spiritual practices
- trauma, violence, or sensitive history
- disability representation
- identity-related themes
- real-world conflict narratives

A sensitivity reader can highlight:

- stereotypes
- careless language
- harmful assumptions
- misrepresentation
- context missing that creates unfair framing

This is not about censorship. This is about responsibility. If my book touches real communities, I want to treat those communities with dignity.

Sensitivity readers are especially valuable when I am writing outside my lived experience or when I am writing about a painful issue that affects many people.

How I Choose a Sensitivity Reader

I choose someone who:

- has lived experience relevant to the content
- understands the genre

- can explain concerns clearly
- can separate harm concerns from personal preference

Sensitivity reading is not the same as ideological approval. A good sensitivity reader does not require me to "agree" with them. They help me avoid avoidable harm and unfairness.

How I Ask Questions That Produce Usable Feedback

The quality of feedback depends heavily on the quality of the questions I ask.

If I ask, "What do you think?" I will get opinions. Opinions are often vague.

If I ask structured questions, I get usable information.

I learned to treat feedback like research. I do not want random reactions. I want data about the reading experience.

Here is how I ask better questions.

1) I Ask for Specific Moments, Not General Feelings

Instead of:

- "Was it good?"

I ask:

- "Where did you feel bored?"
- "Where did you feel confused?"
- "Where did you want to stop reading?"
- "Which chapter felt strongest and why?"
- "Which part felt unnecessary?"

Specific moments reveal real problems.

2) I Ask for a Summary to Test Clarity

One of the best questions is:

- "Summarize this chapter in one sentence."

If the reader cannot summarize it, my chapter is unclear or unfocused.

This is true in fiction and nonfiction.

In fiction, the summary shows whether the plot movement is clear. In nonfiction, it shows whether the lesson is clear.

3) I Ask for Expectations vs Delivery

Reader expectations are the core of satisfaction.

So I ask:

- "What did you expect this book to be about from the opening?"
- "Did the book deliver what you expected?"
- "Did anything feel misleading?"

This helps me align packaging and content.

4) I Ask for Confusion Triggers

When a reader says, "I was confused," I ask a follow-up:

- "What exactly were you confused about?"
- "What did you think was happening?"
- "What did you need to know to understand it?"

Confusion is not always about missing words. Sometimes it is about missing context. Sometimes it is about poor transitions. Sometimes it is about unclear character motivation.

If I understand the confusion trigger, I can fix it.

5) I Ask for Emotional Temperature

Even nonfiction has emotional temperature. The reader's feelings matter.

So I ask:

- "Where did you feel emotionally engaged?"
- "Where did you feel disconnected?"
- "Were there moments that felt forced?"

In memoir and fiction, this is crucial. In nonfiction, it reveals whether examples and stories are landing properly.

6) I Ask for Reader Trust Signals

Trust is invisible until it breaks.

So I ask:

- "At what point did you trust the narrator?"
- "Did anything make you doubt the narrator or the argument?"
- "Did any claim feel exaggerated or unsupported?"

This is one of the most valuable feedback categories because it prevents future bad reviews.

Sorting Feedback: What Is Signal, What Is Preference

Feedback can rescue a book, but it can also confuse me if I treat every comment as equally true.

I learned to sort feedback into categories so I can make wise decisions.

1) Signal: Repeated Patterns Across Multiple Readers

Signal is what repeats.

If three readers mention:

- "Chapter 4 drags,"
- "I was confused in the same scene,"
- "The middle feels repetitive,"

that is signal.

Even if I disagree emotionally, repetition tells me the issue is real. The specific solution may vary, but the problem exists.

Signal is also visible when a reader's reaction matches my own hidden doubts. If a reader names something I secretly feared, that is strong signal.

2) Signal: Confusion and Misinterpretation

If a reader misunderstands my meaning, that is almost always signal.

Even if the reader is "wrong," their misunderstanding reveals my writing did not guide them properly.

I treat misunderstanding as an editing gift. It shows me where clarity is missing.

3) Preference: Personal Taste That Does Not Affect Function

Some feedback is simply taste.

Examples:

- "I don't like first-person narration."
- "I prefer shorter chapters."
- "I don't enjoy this topic."
- "I don't like this type of humor."

These are preferences, not problems, unless my target audience shares the same preference.

If a reader hates my genre, their feedback will not be useful. If a reader dislikes my narrator's personality, that might be okay if my target readers will relate.

So I ask: is this preference common in my audience or unique to this person?

4) Preference: Stylistic Suggestions That Change Voice

Some readers want to rewrite the book. They suggest different words, different tone, different style.

I do not accept these suggestions automatically because they can erase my voice.

If a suggestion improves clarity without changing voice, I consider it. If it changes my voice into theirs, I reject it.

5) Mixed Feedback: Good Diagnosis, Bad Solution

This is the most common category.

A reader says, "This section feels slow. You should delete it."

They may be right about slowness, but deletion may not be the best fix. The real fix might be tightening, moving, or changing the scene's purpose.

So I separate:

- problem identification (often valuable)
- proposed solution (often optional)

I thank readers for spotting problems, but I keep control of solutions.

My Method for Processing Feedback Without Losing My Mind

When feedback arrives, I do not revise immediately. I process first.

Here is my method.

Step 1: I Collect All Feedback in One Place

I create a feedback document or spreadsheet. I list:

- reader name
- chapter/section
- comment summary
- category (clarity, pacing, voice, trust, etc.)

This prevents feedback from becoming scattered.

Step 2: I Look for Patterns

I highlight repeated issues.

- If multiple readers mention the same problem, it becomes priority.

- If only one reader mentions it, I evaluate whether they are in my target audience.

Step 3: I Decide the Level of Fix Needed

Some issues require:

- a structural fix (Pass 1 or Pass 2)
- a line-level fix (Pass 3)
- a mechanics fix (Pass 4)

Feedback often reveals the level of the problem.

Step 4: I Revise in Batches

I do not fix everything randomly. I create a batch plan:

- Batch 1: clarity fixes
- Batch 2: pacing fixes
- Batch 3: voice fixes
- Batch 4: mechanics sweep

This keeps revision controlled.

Practice Section: My Feedback Form (10 Questions That Expose Real Problems)

This is the tool that changed my feedback life. Instead of asking for general opinions, I send a form with clear questions.

I do not need fancy software. This can be a simple document. The power is in the questions.

Here are my 10 questions.

My 10-Question Feedback Form

1) What do you think this book is about (in one sentence)?
This tests whether the promise is clear.

2) What did you expect after reading the first chapter, and did the rest deliver that expectation?
This tests delivery and trust.

3) Where did you feel confused, and what exactly were you confused about?
This reveals clarity gaps.

4) Where did you feel bored or tempted to skim, and why?
This reveals pacing problems.

5) Which chapter or section felt strongest, and what made it strong?
This shows what is working and should be protected.

6) Which chapter or section felt weakest, and what made it weak?
This reveals structural or focus problems.

7) Did anything feel repetitive? If yes, where?
This reveals redundancy and over-explaining.

8) Did the narrator/author voice feel consistent? If not, where did it shift?
This reveals tone and voice problems.

9) Did any claim, scene, or moment make you doubt the book's credibility or fairness?
This reveals trust breaks.

10) If you could change one thing to improve this book for readers like you, what would it be?
This reveals high-impact priorities.

Optional Add-On Questions (If Needed)

If I need more targeted feedback, I add one or two questions specific to my genre:

- For fiction: "Were the character motivations believable? Where not?"
- For nonfiction: "Were the steps actionable? Where did you want more examples?"
- For memoir: "Were there moments that felt emotionally forced or unclear?"
- For academic: "Were the definitions and logic chain clear? Where did evidence feel thin?"

But I keep the core form to 10 questions so readers will complete it.

Closing Thought for Chapter 9

Collaboration is not about collecting praise. Collaboration is about reducing blindness.

Beta readers help me test the reader experience.
Critique partners help me sharpen craft and structure.
Sensitivity readers help me protect fairness and dignity.

But none of these work well unless I ask disciplined questions and sort feedback wisely.

When I learn to separate signal from preference, feedback becomes fuel, not confusion. It becomes a practical tool that strengthens the manuscript without stealing my voice.

A book improves when I stop editing alone in my head and start testing my work in the real world of readers. That is what professional authors do. They do not guess. They measure. They revise. They serve the reader.

CHAPTER 10: FORMATTING AS PART OF EDITING (BECAUSE LAYOUT CREATES NEW ERRORS)

For years, I thought formatting was a separate job, something I did after editing was "done." I treated formatting like packaging. I assumed that once the words were correct, I could simply pour them into a template and publish.

Then I learned the hard way: formatting is not only packaging. Formatting is part of editing, because layout creates new errors.

A clean manuscript can become messy after layout. A sentence that looked fine in a Word document can break awkwardly on a printed page. A heading can lose its hierarchy. A list can misalign. A table can collapse. A link can break. A paragraph style can drift. A missing page break can destroy the professional look of an entire chapter.

That is why I do not call the book finished until I proof the formatted version. The formatted version is what the reader will experience. If I proof only the raw manuscript, I am checking a product the reader will never see.

So this chapter is about treating formatting as a quality stage, not a cosmetic stage. It is about understanding the basics that prevent problems and using a final "after layout" proof to catch what formatting introduces.

Why I Do a Final Proof Only After Formatting

Proofreading before formatting is useful, but it is not final. It is early proof.

Final proof must happen after formatting because formatting changes the reading surface in several ways.

1) Formatting Reveals Hidden Errors

Some errors hide inside a normal document view:

- double spaces become obvious in print
- inconsistent indentation becomes visible
- heading inconsistencies stand out
- awkward line breaks reveal sentence weaknesses
- repeated words appear when the eye moves slower on a page

When a book is formatted, it looks like a book. The mind reads differently. The eyes catch different things.

That is why many authors find errors in their print proof that they missed in the manuscript file. It is not because they became smarter overnight. It is because the surface changed.

2) Formatting Can Introduce New Problems

Formatting can create problems that did not exist before:

- missing or duplicated words during file conversion
- broken italics or bold
- strange hyphenation
- extra spaces at paragraph starts
- lists that lose alignment
- page breaks in the wrong places
- orphan lines or widowed lines
- table of contents errors
- missing images or mis-sized images
- broken links in ebooks
- inconsistent fonts or font sizes
- inconsistent spacing before headings

Even if my manuscript is clean, conversion and layout can create errors.

3) Reader Experience Happens in the Layout

A book is not only words. It is also navigation and comfort.

The reader experiences:

- chapter openings
- page turns
- heading structure
- list readability
- spacing
- typography consistency

If these feel sloppy, the reader will trust the book less, even if the writing itself is strong.

So I treat formatting as part of quality.

4) The "Final" Version Is the Proof Version

The most important truth: the formatted proof is the final product.

If I do not proof that final product, I am gambling with my reputation.

So my rule is:

No matter what, I do a final proof after layout.

Even if I am on a tight schedule, I do it. It is the last gate.

Manuscript Basics: Trim Size, Margins, Paragraph Styles, Headings

Formatting feels intimidating when I treat it like graphic design. But at the core, book formatting is about consistent structure.

If I understand the basics, I prevent most problems before they start.

1) Trim Size: The Shape of the Book

Trim size is the physical size of the printed book. It affects:

- margin requirements
- line length
- page count
- readability
- cost of printing
- spine thickness

Different genres lean toward different trim sizes.

A workbook or textbook might use a larger trim for space.
A novel often uses standard paperback sizes.
A guide may use a size that feels comfortable for reference.

The key lesson is this: trim size influences layout. If I change trim size late, the whole book layout shifts. That shift can create errors.

So I decide trim size before final formatting.

2) Margins: Reader Comfort and Print Safety

Margins are not decoration. Margins protect the reader.

In print, margins must account for:

- binding (the gutter)
- printing variance
- comfortable reading space

If margins are too tight, the book feels cheap and hard to read. If the gutter margin is too small, words disappear into the binding.

So I choose margins based on:

- trim size
- page count
- binding type

The principle is simple: give the reader breathing room. A book is not meant to feel cramped.

3) Paragraph Styles: The Secret Weapon of Clean Formatting

The most powerful formatting concept is paragraph styles.

A style is a formatting rule applied consistently:

- body text style
- heading styles
- subheading styles
- block quote styles
- list styles

If I format manually, I will create inconsistency. I will forget. I will drift.

If I use styles, the book becomes consistent automatically.

Styles help me:

- keep font and size consistent
- keep spacing consistent
- maintain indentation rules
- maintain heading hierarchy
- generate a table of contents properly
- update the whole book quickly if needed

This is why a clean manuscript should be style-based, not manually formatted line by line.

4) Headings: The Navigation System of the Book

Headings are how readers navigate. In nonfiction especially, headings matter deeply. Readers often skim and scan before reading. They decide whether the book is useful by looking at headings.

Headings must be consistent:

- same font treatment
- same spacing
- same hierarchy
- same capitalization style

I choose a heading system:

- Chapter titles (top level)
- Major section headings (level 2)
- Minor subheadings (level 3)

Then I apply it consistently.

In ebooks, headings are even more important because they affect navigation and table of contents structure.

Lists, Tables, Images, and Front/Back Matter Consistency

Now we move into the areas where formatting and editing collide strongly. These elements are where readers notice sloppiness fast.

1) Lists: Bullets and Numbered Steps

Lists are common in nonfiction, but they also appear in fiction and memoir when the narrator lists items for effect.

List problems include:

- inconsistent punctuation at the end of bullet points
- inconsistent capitalization (some bullets start with caps, others with lowercase)
- inconsistent parallel structure (one bullet is a phrase, another is a full sentence)
- inconsistent indentation
- uneven spacing between bullets
- mixed numbering styles

My approach is to decide list rules early:

- Do bullets end with periods? Only if they are full sentences.
- Are list items parallel in structure?
- Are numbered steps written as commands?

I also ensure lists are not too long without break. Long lists become walls.

2) Tables: Structure and Readability

Tables can look great or terrible depending on formatting.

Table problems include:

- text too small to read
- columns that break across pages awkwardly
- inconsistent alignment
- tables that do not convert well to ebook formats
- missing labels or unclear headings

If I use tables, I keep them simple. I label them clearly. I test them in the final formats.

For ebooks, I remember: tables are risky. Many ebook readers display tables poorly. So if a table is essential, I consider converting it into a list or a series of short blocks that reflow better.

3) Images: Placement, Resolution, and Captions

Images introduce many errors.

Image issues include:

- low resolution causing blur in print
- wrong color mode leading to dull print results
- images too close to margins
- captions inconsistent in style
- images placed inconsistently relative to text
- images breaking page flow awkwardly

I make image rules:

- consistent placement (centered, full width, or aligned)
- consistent caption style (font, size, spacing)
- consistent labeling if needed ("Figure 1", "Figure 2")

And I always check print resolution. A good image on screen can look terrible in print.

4) Front Matter Consistency

Front matter includes elements like:

- dedication
- acknowledgments
- table of contents
- foreword or preface (if included)

Even if front matter is short, it must be consistent with the rest of the book:

- consistent typography
- consistent spacing
- consistent heading treatment

A common error is having front matter styled differently from the body because the author copied it from another template.

I check front matter carefully because it is the reader's first impression.

5) Back Matter Consistency

Back matter includes:

- final note
- review request
- copies/bulk orders info
- about the author
- book descriptions
- other books list

Back matter must also be consistent:

- headings aligned with chapter heading style
- spacing consistent
- links correct (especially in ebook)
- email/website text correct

Back matter errors are painful because they often involve contact details and links. If I publish a broken link, I lose opportunities.

Practice Section: My "Print-Ready" and "Ebook-Ready" Checks

This practice section is my final gate. I use two checklists: one for print, one for ebook. Even if the manuscript is the same, the format checks differ.

The goal is simple: the formatted product must be clean and comfortable for the reader.

My Print-Ready Checklist

A) Layout and Structure

- Chapter starts on the correct side if required (commonly right-hand pages).
- Chapter title formatting is consistent across all chapters.
- Page numbers are correct and positioned consistently.
- No missing page numbers.
- Headers and footers (if used) are consistent and correct.
- Section breaks and page breaks are intentional, not accidental.

B) Margins and Gutter

- Margins are wide enough for comfortable reading.
- Gutter margin is sufficient for binding.
- Text does not disappear into the binding.
- No text too close to page edges.

C) Typography and Spacing

- Body font is consistent throughout.
- Font size is readable for the genre.
- Line spacing is consistent.
- Paragraph indentation is consistent.
- No random extra spaces between paragraphs unless intentionally used.
- Orphans and widows are minimized (no lonely single lines at top or bottom of pages).

D) Headings and Lists

- Headings follow a consistent hierarchy.
- Spacing before and after headings is consistent.
- Lists are aligned properly.
- Bullets and numbers are consistent in style.

- List punctuation rules are consistent.

E) Images and Tables

- Images are high enough resolution for print.
- Captions are consistent.
- Images are placed consistently and do not break margins.
- Tables are readable and do not split awkwardly across pages.
- Any figure labels match in style.

F) Front and Back Matter

- Table of contents matches page numbers accurately (if used).
- Dedication and other front matter are correctly placed.
- Back matter headings match the book style.
- Contact details are correct.

G) Final Proof Habits

- I proof on the actual PDF, not the Word file.
- I read slowly, line by line in key sections.
- I check the first 10 pages extra carefully (first impression zone).
- I check the last 10 pages extra carefully (closing credibility zone).

My Ebook-Ready Checklist

A) Navigation

- Table of contents works and links correctly.
- Chapter navigation works in the device previewer.
- Headings appear properly in the ebook table of contents.
- No missing chapters in navigation.

B) Reflow and Readability

- Text reflows cleanly on different font sizes.
- Paragraph breaks behave correctly.
- Indentation and spacing remain consistent.
- No weird line breaks caused by manual formatting.

C) Headings and Hierarchy

- Chapter titles are consistent.
- Section headings are consistent.
- Heading levels are used properly (no random style shifts).

D) Lists

- Lists display correctly across devices.
- Bullet and number formatting remains consistent.
- No list items broken by strange spacing.

E) Links and References

- All hyperlinks work (email, website, internal links).
- No raw URLs that look ugly unless needed.
- Any footnotes/endnotes work if included.

F) Images

- Images are sized appropriately for e-readers.
- Images do not overflow or distort.
- Captions remain tied to images properly.

G) Front and Back Matter

- Front matter displays correctly in ebook format.
- Back matter is easy to navigate.
- Review request and author info are easy to find.
- Links in back matter are correct.

H) Final Proof Habits

- I test on at least two device views (phone and tablet/desktop preview).
- I scan for formatting glitches that do not appear in Word.
- I check the first chapter and last chapter especially carefully.

My Final Formatting Rule: Never Trust a Single View

One view can hide errors. A PDF can look fine on a laptop but reveal issues on a phone. An ebook can look fine in one previewer but glitch on a different device.

So I always test in more than one view when possible.

Closing Thought for Chapter 10

Formatting is not only visual. Formatting is editorial because it shapes how the reader receives the text. Layout can introduce errors and expose weaknesses. That is why the final proof must happen after formatting, not before.

When I treat formatting as part of editing, I protect my reader from distractions. I protect my book from embarrassment. I protect my name from careless mistakes.

A book is not finished when the words are written. A book is finished when the reader can move through it smoothly, from the first page to the last, without tripping over errors that should have been caught.

That is what professionalism looks like in indie publishing: a clean manuscript, a clean layout, and a final proof that respects the real product the reader will hold in their hands.

CHAPTER 11: COVER AND BOOK PACKAGING (EDITING THE FIRST IMPRESSION)

When I first started publishing, I thought my cover was a decoration. I treated it like clothing: something to make the book look "nice." I believed the writing would carry everything else.

Then reality taught me a brutal truth: readers judge before they read.

The cover is not just a picture. The cover is the first edit the reader performs on my book. They scan it and decide whether my book belongs in their world. They decide whether I look professional. They decide whether my promise is believable. They decide whether they will click.

In indie publishing, the cover is often the difference between a book that is ignored and a book that gets a chance. That means cover work is part of editing. Not editing words, but editing perception.

This chapter is about editing the first impression. It is about understanding what a cover must communicate, avoiding the mistakes that sabotage trust, and using a repeatable process that produces a strong cover without endless guessing.

What a Cover Must Communicate: Genre, Promise, Professionalism

A good cover does three jobs at once. If it fails any one of these jobs, the book loses sales and credibility.

1) Genre: "What Kind of Experience Is This?"

Genre is the first question the reader asks. They ask it in half a second.

The cover answers:

- Is this romance or thriller?
- Is this memoir or business guide?
- Is this fantasy or literary fiction?
- Is this academic work or popular nonfiction?

If my cover does not communicate genre, the reader feels confused. Confused readers do not buy. They move on.

Genre communication happens through:

- typography style
- color palette
- imagery
- composition
- visual tone

A thriller often uses darker tones, tension cues, sharp typography.
A romance often uses softer palettes, warmth, intimacy cues.
A business book often uses clean design, bold typography, simple visuals.
A memoir often uses a human element, emotional tone, and a credible, respectful design.

I do not copy other covers, but I study genre signals. The goal is not to be original at the cost of being unreadable. The goal is to be clear first, distinctive second.

2) Promise: "What Will This Book Do for Me?"

The cover also communicates promise, especially in nonfiction.

Promise is:

- the transformation
- the solution

- the result

A nonfiction cover must tell the reader what the book helps them achieve.

Promise is communicated through:

- title wording
- subtitle wording
- design hierarchy (what is emphasized)
- symbols or imagery that suggests the outcome

If my title is vague and my subtitle is missing, the promise becomes unclear. The reader cannot justify buying.

In fiction, promise is the emotional experience:

- suspense
- wonder
- comfort
- excitement
- depth

The cover hints at that emotional promise through tone and visuals.

3) Professionalism: "Can I Trust This Author?"

Professionalism is the silent requirement.

A cover that looks amateur signals an amateur book. Even if the writing is strong, the reader will assume the inside is sloppy. This is not always fair, but it is real.

Professionalism is communicated through:

- clean typography

- spacing and alignment
- consistent hierarchy
- good image quality
- correct genre signals
- restraint and focus

A professional cover looks intentional. It looks like it belongs on a shelf next to other books in the category.

Professional does not mean expensive. It means disciplined.

Common Cover Mistakes I Avoid

Once I learned what covers must communicate, I started noticing common mistakes that sabotage books. These mistakes are not minor. They destroy trust.

Here are the mistakes I avoid.

1) Clutter

Clutter happens when I try to show everything. I add multiple images, multiple fonts, multiple decorative elements, and too much text.

Clutter confuses the eye. The reader cannot find the title quickly. The cover becomes noise.

A clean cover usually has:

- one dominant focal point
- one clear typography system
- one message

The cover is not a poster. It is a signal.

When I feel tempted to add more, I ask: what is the one thing the cover must say? Then I remove everything that does not serve that.

2) Unreadable Fonts

Unreadable fonts are one of the biggest indie cover killers. If the reader cannot read the title in a thumbnail, the cover has failed.

Common font problems include:

- thin fonts with low contrast
- overly decorative fonts that are hard to read
- fonts that do not match the genre
- too many fonts mixed together
- poor spacing between letters

I follow a simple rule:

If the title is not readable at thumbnail size, the design is not done.

Readability is not optional. It is the price of entry.

3) Too Much Text

Some authors treat the cover like a sales page. They add:

- long subtitles
- multiple taglines
- several claims and promises
- lists of benefits

This creates crowding and kills hierarchy.

A cover should not explain everything. The cover should create a clear promise and invite the reader to learn more in the description.

I keep the cover text minimal:

- title
- subtitle (if needed)
- author name
- series name or category line (optional)

That is enough for most books.

4) Weak Hierarchy

Hierarchy means the order in which the eye reads elements.

A weak hierarchy happens when:

- the subtitle is bigger than the title
- the author name competes with the title
- the imagery fights the text
- multiple elements are the same weight

A strong hierarchy answers:

- What do I see first?
- What do I see second?
- What do I see third?

Usually:

1. Title
2. Subtitle or key concept image
3. Author name

But the order can shift depending on the book. The key is that it must be intentional.

5) Low-Quality Images

A low-resolution image, a stretched image, or a poorly cut-out object instantly signals amateur work.

I avoid:

- pixelated images
- overly compressed images
- mismatched lighting between elements
- obvious stock photo clichés without transformation
- poor cropping

If I use stock images, I treat them with respect. I do not just drop them in. I color grade them, adjust contrast, and make them fit the design.

6) Genre Confusion

A cover can be clean and still fail if it signals the wrong genre.

For example:

- a romance cover that looks like a thriller
- a business cover that looks like a fantasy novel
- a memoir cover that looks like a cookbook

Genre confusion attracts the wrong readers and repels the right ones. This creates bad reviews because the book was marketed incorrectly.

So genre alignment is part of my editing.

7) Inconsistent Series Branding

If I write a series, the covers must look like a family.

If my covers look unrelated, readers do not recognize the series. I lose repeat buyers.

Series consistency includes:

- consistent typography choices
- consistent layout structure
- consistent palette logic
- consistent placement of series name and author name

Consistency does not mean repetition. It means recognizable identity.

My Process: Concept, Hierarchy, Thumbnail Test, Iteration

A good cover is rarely born in one attempt. It is produced through a clean process.

This is the process I use. It is repeatable. It reduces guesswork.

Step 1: I Define the Cover Concept

The concept is the single visual idea that represents the book.

In nonfiction, concept often represents transformation or solution.

Examples:

- a blueprint graphic for a skills book
- a compass for guidance
- a ladder for progress
- a clean icon representing the main tool

In fiction, concept often represents atmosphere, stakes, or world.

Examples:

- a shadowy figure for mystery
- a symbolic object for literary fiction
- a landscape hint for fantasy
- a dramatic lighting cue for thriller

I do not start with images. I start with concept.

I write:

- "This cover should feel like ____."
- "This cover should communicate ____."
- "The symbol of this book is ____."

If I cannot describe the concept clearly, my design will drift.

Step 2: I Establish Hierarchy

Before I choose fonts, I decide what must dominate.

I decide:

- what is the largest element (usually title)
- what supports it (subtitle or image)
- what is secondary (author name, series line)

Hierarchy decisions make design easier because they limit options.

Step 3: I Choose Typography That Matches Genre

Typography is not decoration. Typography carries emotion and authority.

I choose fonts that match the category:

- bold serif or clean sans for business and professional nonfiction

- softer serif or script accents for certain romance subgenres (carefully)
- sharp sans or condensed bold for thrillers
- elegant serif for literary or memoir, depending on tone

I avoid using too many fonts.

Most strong covers use:

- one font family with multiple weights, or
- two fonts that complement each other

Too many fonts create chaos.

Step 4: I Build the First Draft Cover Fast

I do not aim for perfection on draft one. I aim for structure.

I place:

- title
- subtitle
- author name
- primary image or symbol

Then I ensure:

- clear contrast
- readable text
- balanced spacing

Draft one is a skeleton. It is meant to be improved.

Step 5: I Do a Thumbnail Test

This is the test most indie authors skip, and it costs them sales.

I shrink the cover to thumbnail size and ask:

- Can I read the title?
- Can I sense the genre?
- Does it look professional in small size?

If the title disappears, I increase contrast, simplify backgrounds, and increase font weight.

If the cover looks muddy, I simplify.

If the cover feels confusing, I remove elements.

The thumbnail test forces clarity.

Step 6: I Run a Shelf Test

The shelf test is where I compare my cover to other covers in the category. I place my cover next to bestsellers and strong mid-list books and ask:

- Does my cover belong?
- Does it look cheap compared to others?
- Does it signal the same genre?
- Does it have a clear concept?

This test is not about copying. It is about avoiding amateur signals.

Step 7: I Iterate With Discipline

Iteration is improvement through controlled change.

I change one variable at a time:

- font weight
- spacing
- background darkness

- image placement
- color palette
- subtitle length

If I change five things at once, I cannot learn what helped.

Iteration is how a cover becomes sharp.

Step 8: I Proof the Cover Like a Manuscript

A cover can be beautiful and still fail because of small errors:

- misspelled author name
- inconsistent capitalization
- wrong subtitle punctuation
- misaligned text
- inconsistent series numbering

So I proof the cover:

- title spelling
- subtitle spelling
- author name spelling
- series line consistency
- alignment checks

The cover must be as clean as the manuscript.

Book Packaging Beyond the Cover

The cover is the front door, but packaging includes more than the cover. Packaging is the full first impression system:

- title and subtitle
- series name and positioning
- book description
- typography inside the book

- trim size and paper choice for print
- formatting style
- author brand consistency

A strong cover paired with weak packaging still struggles.

This is why I treat packaging like editing: it must be consistent, credible, and aligned with reader expectations.

Practice Section: I Write a One-Sentence Cover Brief and a 5-Word Mood Line

This practice is simple but powerful. It forces clarity. It gives me something concrete to share with a designer, and it keeps me focused if I design the cover myself.

1) My One-Sentence Cover Brief Template

I write one sentence that includes:

- genre
- target reader
- promise
- tone

Here is the template:

"Design a cover for a [genre/category] book for [target reader] that promises [result/experience] and feels [tone words]."

Example (Nonfiction Editing Guide)

"Design a cover for a practical indie publishing guide for self-publishing authors that promises a clean, professional manuscript and feels clear, confident, and disciplined."

That one sentence becomes my north star.

2) My 5-Word Mood Line

Mood is emotional direction. I choose five words that describe how the cover should feel.

Examples:

- "Clean. Confident. Practical. Modern. Trustworthy."
- "Dark. Suspenseful. Sharp. Dangerous. Fast."
- "Warm. Honest. Human. Reflective. Hopeful."
- "Scholarly. Precise. Serious. Structured. Credible."

The mood line prevents me from drifting into random design decisions.

Why Only Five Words

Because too many words become confusion. Five words force me to choose the true identity of the cover.

3) How I Use the Brief and Mood Line

I use them to:

- guide my own design work
- guide a designer
- evaluate iterations
- avoid clutter
- protect genre clarity

If a design choice contradicts the mood line, it probably does not belong.

Closing Thought for Chapter 11

A cover is not a decoration. It is a promise at a glance.

A strong cover communicates:

- genre,
- promise,
- professionalism.

It avoids clutter, unreadable fonts, and text overload. It uses clear hierarchy, strong contrast, and a clean concept. It passes the thumbnail test. It fits the shelf without disappearing.

Most importantly, a strong cover respects the reader's decision process. Readers do not owe my book time. My cover must earn the click.

When I treat the cover as part of editing, I stop thinking like a hobbyist and start thinking like a publisher. I edit the first impression so the reader will give the words inside a fair chance.

CHAPTER 12: PUBLISHING AND MARKETING TOOLS I USE AFTER THE MANUSCRIPT IS CLEAN

I used to believe publishing was the finish line. I thought the hard work ended when the manuscript was edited, proofed, and formatted. I would upload the files, click publish, and hope the world would notice.

Then I learned what every indie publisher eventually learns: publishing is not the end. Publishing is the beginning of distribution.

A clean manuscript is the foundation. But readers do not discover books because they are clean. Readers discover books because the packaging and the marketplace signals help them find what they want. If I publish a clean book with messy metadata, weak description, wrong categories, and no plan, I have built a good product and placed it in a dark corner.

This chapter is about what I do after the manuscript is clean. It is about the tools and checks I use to publish professionally, test marketing intelligently, and maintain my book after launch.

I do not treat this stage as hype. I treat it as hygiene. Good publishing hygiene protects my book from avoidable mistakes and gives it a fair chance in the marketplace.

KDP Basics: What I Set Up and What I Double-Check Before Publishing

KDP is simple on the surface, but small mistakes here create big problems later. I treat the KDP upload process like a final checklist, not like a form to rush through.

Here is what I set up and what I double-check.

1) I Confirm the Core Files Are Correct

Before I even open KDP, I confirm:

- I am uploading the final formatted interior file (not an older draft).
- I am uploading the correct cover file for the right trim size.
- The cover includes the correct spine width (print).
- The interior file has correct front and back matter.
- The table of contents is correct.
- My author name is spelled correctly and consistently across the book and cover.

This sounds basic, but many authors publish wrong versions because they rush.

I do not rush.

2) I Confirm Format-Specific Details

For Print

I confirm:

- trim size matches the interior file
- margins and gutter are correct
- page count makes sense for spine width
- bleed settings match the cover design
- the barcode area is correct (if KDP adds it)

I also check that the cover text remains readable and aligned after KDP preview.

For Ebook

I confirm:

- navigation works
- table of contents links work
- headings appear correctly in the Kindle TOC
- images display properly
- the ebook preview looks clean on multiple simulated devices

If my ebook looks good only in one preview mode, it is not ready.

3) I Set Up Book Details With Discipline

This is where many indie authors fail. The book details are not decoration. They are the book's search and sales foundation.

Title and Subtitle

I check:

- correct capitalization
- consistent subtitle usage across cover and listing
- no keyword stuffing that makes the title look ridiculous
- clarity over cleverness

Series Information

If the book is part of a series, I make sure:

- series name is consistent across all books
- series numbering is correct
- series format is consistent (Book 1, Book 2, etc. if used)

Series mistakes break the reader journey and reduce read-through.

Author Name

I ensure:

- the author name matches what readers will search
- it matches my other books
- it matches the name on the cover and interior

Even a small mismatch can split my author page or confuse indexing.

4) I Choose Categories Carefully

Categories are not just labels. They influence discoverability.

I choose categories based on:

- true genre fit
- reader expectation fit
- competition realism

I avoid categories that are too broad if my book is niche. I also avoid categories that mislead the reader.

Misleading categories create bad reviews because readers feel tricked.

5) I Choose Keywords With Intent

Keywords help readers find my book. But the goal is not to cram keywords everywhere. The goal is relevance.

I choose keywords based on:

- what my reader would search
- what problem they want solved
- how they describe their desire in real language

I avoid:

- irrelevant keywords for traffic

- misleading keywords for ranking
- hype claims I cannot support

A clean book deserves honest metadata.

6) I Set Pricing With Strategy

Pricing is not only money. Pricing is positioning.

I consider:

- book length
- genre norms
- my brand stage (new author vs established)
- whether I want rapid volume or higher royalty per sale
- whether I will run promotions later

I also check print costs. Print pricing must leave room for royalty. Pricing too low can produce tiny royalties or none.

For ebooks, I consider pricing flexibility because promotional strategies can use temporary discounts.

7) I Use KDP Preview Tools Like a Quality Gate

The KDP previewer is not optional.

I use it to check:

- cover placement
- spine alignment
- margins
- weird formatting issues
- page breaks
- header/footer consistency

I do not assume my exported file is perfect. I test it in KDP preview.

8) I Order a Print Proof When Possible

If I can, I order a print proof. Nothing replaces holding the book.

A print proof reveals:

- paper feel and readability
- margin comfort
- image quality
- cover color differences
- spine text alignment
- tiny errors I missed on screen

If I cannot order a proof, I at least review the PDF carefully and zoom in on key areas.

My rule: if print matters to me, proof matters too.

Amazon Ads Basics: Why Small Tests Beat Big Guesses

Advertising can waste money fast. Many authors either avoid ads completely or burn cash without learning.

I choose a disciplined approach: small tests that teach me.

Ads do not create a good book. Ads amplify what is already good. If the cover, description, and book quality are weak, ads will not save it. They will just accelerate disappointment.

So I run ads only after my foundation is clean.

1) Why I Prefer Small Tests

Small tests protect my budget and produce real information.

A big ad spend with no testing is gambling. A small test is research.

With small tests, I can answer:

- Which keywords convert?
- Which categories of targeting work?
- Does my cover attract clicks?
- Does my description convert?
- Is my pricing positioned correctly?

Small tests help me diagnose the weakest link.

2) The Main Pieces of Amazon Ads I Respect

Even without going deep into advanced tactics, I respect three basics:

- targeting
- bid control
- conversion tracking mindset

Targeting

I think in three simple lanes:

- keyword targeting (what readers search)
- product targeting (books similar to mine)
- category targeting (placing my book in a browsing lane)

If my book is niche, product targeting can work well because the reader is already in a relevant shopping mood.

Bid Control

I avoid overbidding early. My goal is data, not dominance.

I start modest. I let the system collect impressions and clicks. Then I adjust.

Conversion Mindset

If clicks happen but sales do not, ads are not the problem. The listing is the problem.

Ads reveal the truth:

- clicks without sales often mean weak cover-title-subtitle match or weak description
- impressions without clicks often mean weak cover or weak targeting relevance

Ads are diagnostic tools if I treat them that way.

3) What I Watch First

In early testing, I watch:

- clicks
- spend
- sales attributed to ads (where possible)
- cost per click patterns
- which targets produce meaningful engagement

I am not chasing perfection. I am learning what works.

My Launch Hygiene: Description, Keywords, Categories, Pricing, Reviews Plan

Many authors think launch is a day. I treat launch as a system. The day matters, but the hygiene matters more.

Launch hygiene is what I prepare so the book has stable market signals.

1) Description: My Sales Page in Plain Text

The description is not a summary. It is a conversion tool.

A strong description does three jobs:

- It clarifies who the book is for.
- It clarifies what problem it solves or what experience it delivers.
- It reduces reader doubt and creates confidence.

I avoid a description that rambles like a back-cover blurb with no structure. I also avoid a description filled with exaggerated claims.

Instead, I aim for:

- a strong opening hook aligned with the promise
- clear reader problem identification
- clear benefits
- a short list of what the reader will learn or experience (if nonfiction)
- a closing that invites action

I also keep the description consistent with the cover promise. If the cover says "practical guide," the description must feel practical.

2) Keywords: Relevance Over Tricks

I do not treat keywords as magic. I treat them as accuracy.

I choose phrases the reader actually types.

For a book like an editing guide, relevant searches might be:

- self-editing checklist
- copyediting for authors
- proofreading tips for books

- how to edit a manuscript
- editing process for self-publishing

I avoid:

- irrelevant high-traffic keywords
- confusing mixed-genre signals
- keywords that promise something the book does not deliver

Relevance produces better reviews because readers get what they came for.

3) Categories: Match the Reader's Shelf

Categories must reflect the reader's mental shelf.

If my book is a practical guide for indie authors, I do not place it in a category that suggests it is a memoir. If my book is a memoir, I do not place it in a business category.

I aim for:

- category alignment
- competition realism
- reader expectation accuracy

This protects my reviews. People get angry when they buy a book expecting one thing and receive another.

4) Pricing: A Clean Offer

Pricing affects perception.

Too low can signal low value. Too high can repel new readers.

I consider:

- my genre norms
- book length
- brand stage
- whether I will use promos

I also keep my pricing stable during the early days so I can evaluate performance accurately. Constant price changes create noise in my data.

5) Reviews Plan: How I Approach It Ethically

Reviews matter, but they must be earned honestly.

My review plan includes:

- identifying early readers who genuinely want the book
- inviting them to leave honest reviews
- making the request simple and respectful

I avoid:

- review manipulation
- pressure
- fake reviews
- anything that violates platform rules

If my book is good and my audience is real, reviews will come over time. My job is to make it easy for readers who loved the book to share their experience.

I also include a gentle review request inside the book, usually in the back matter, because that is where readers are most likely to respond after finishing.

Practice Section: My Simple Post-Launch Routine (Weekly Checks and Updates)

This practice section is my real secret. Many authors launch and then disappear. Others obsess daily and burn out. I choose a middle path: weekly routine.

A weekly post-launch routine keeps the book healthy without consuming my life.

Here is what I do.

My Weekly Post-Launch Routine

1) I Check My Listing Like a Reader

I visit the book page and check:

- cover display (does it still look strong?)
- title and subtitle clarity
- description formatting (no weird breaks)
- author name consistency
- category placement (still correct?)
- price (still what I intended?)

Sometimes platforms change display formats. I catch issues early.

2) I Check Reviews and Reader Feedback

I look for:

- repeated praise (what is working)
- repeated complaints (what needs improvement)
- confusion signals (description mismatch, category mismatch, content issues)

I do not argue with reviews. I study them.

If readers repeat the same complaint, I treat it as signal. I decide whether I can fix it in an update.

3) I Track Simple Performance Signals

I keep it simple. I track:

- sales numbers (rough trend)
- page reads if in programs that report them
- ad spend vs results (if running ads)
- conversion signals from my own platform traffic (if applicable)

I do not need complex dashboards. I need trend awareness.

4) I Evaluate Ads (If Running)

If I run Amazon Ads, I review:

- which targets are spending without results
- which targets are producing sales or engagement
- whether my bids need small adjustments
- whether I should pause weak targets

My goal is to cut waste and scale what works.

Small improvements weekly create big improvements over time.

5) I Make One Listing Improvement Per Week

I do not overhaul everything constantly. I choose one improvement.

Possible improvements:

- tighten description opening lines
- adjust keyword set if clearly irrelevant

- refine categories if misaligned
- update author bio to match brand
- update A+ content if available (where appropriate)
- adjust pricing if the market response suggests it

One improvement per week keeps momentum without chaos.

6) I Maintain the Manuscript Like a Product

If a reader spots a typo or formatting glitch, I log it.

Once enough small issues accumulate, I prepare a clean update:

- fix typos
- fix formatting problems
- fix broken links in back matter
- update back matter if needed (new books list)

Then I upload the updated files.

This is one advantage of indie publishing: I can improve the product.

But I do not update constantly. I batch updates.

7) I Keep a Simple "Book Health Log"

I keep a document with:

- date
- change made
- reason
- result observed

This prevents me from repeating mistakes and helps me learn what moves the needle.

A Sample Weekly Checklist (Copy and Use)

Weekly Book Hygiene Checklist

- Check book listing display and formatting
- Check reviews and note repeated feedback
- Track basic sales/reads trend
- Review ad targets and pause waste
- Make one listing improvement
- Log any errors for future manuscript update
- Update health log with actions taken

That is enough. Consistency beats intensity.

Closing Thought for Chapter 12

The manuscript is the foundation. But publishing success requires more than a clean manuscript. It requires clean metadata, clean packaging, and disciplined post-launch maintenance.

KDP setup is where I prevent avoidable mistakes.
Amazon Ads are where I learn through small tests instead of big guesses.
Launch hygiene is where I align description, keywords, categories, pricing, and reviews plan.
Post-launch routine is where I keep the book healthy and improving.

This is what it means to publish like a system. I do not rely on luck. I rely on clean work, careful testing, and steady maintenance.

A book is not only written once. It is managed, refined, and positioned so it can reach the readers it was meant to serve.

CHAPTER 13: THE FINAL QUALITY GATE (MY PRE-PUBLISH CHECKLIST)

There is a dangerous moment in indie publishing that no one warns me about loudly enough. It is not the first draft. It is not even the messy middle. It is the moment right before I hit publish, when I feel tired, proud, and impatient.

That is the moment quality dies.

When I am close to the finish line, I start bargaining with myself:

- "It's good enough."
- "Readers won't notice."
- "I'll fix it later."
- "I've already spent too much time on this."

This is where the final quality gate saves me.

A quality gate is a deliberate pause where I stop editing randomly and start checking systematically. It is the difference between a book that is clean and a book that is almost clean. Almost clean is what earns bad reviews.

This chapter is my final gate. It is the checklist and method I use to protect reader trust, catch last-minute errors, and sign off with confidence. It is not about perfection. It is about professionalism.

Why a Final Quality Gate Matters

A reader does not enter my book with mercy. They enter with expectation.

They paid money or time. They expect competence. If they find obvious errors early, they stop trusting me. And once trust breaks, everything else I say feels weaker.

That is why the final quality gate is not a nice ritual. It is a business requirement. My book is a product. If I ship a product with defects, customers complain.

In traditional publishing, multiple departments catch issues. In indie publishing, I am the department.

So I do what real publishers do: I enforce a final gate.

The "Reader Trust" Checklist: Consistency, Clarity, Credibility, Typos, Layout

Reader trust is built on five pillars. When I check these pillars deliberately, I catch most of what matters.

1) Consistency: Does Everything Match Itself?

Consistency is the invisible glue of professionalism. Readers may not praise it, but they notice when it breaks.

My Consistency Checks

Names and Terms

- Character names spelled the same every time
- Place names consistent
- Key terms consistent
- Acronyms defined once and used consistently

Timeline and Facts

- Dates match
- Ages match
- Sequence of events makes sense
- Cause and effect is consistent

Point of View and Tense

- POV does not drift without intention
- Tense does not shift randomly

Style Rules

- Capitalization consistent
- Number formatting consistent (e.g., "10" vs "ten" based on my style choice)
- Italics/bold rules consistent
- Quotation formatting consistent

Headings and Structure

- Chapter headings styled consistently
- Subheadings follow hierarchy
- Spacing before and after headings consistent

Consistency is not glamour work, but it is trust work.

2) Clarity: Can the Reader Follow Without Guessing?

Clarity means the reader understands what I mean the first time, without rereading.

My Clarity Checks

Chapter Purpose

- Each chapter has a clear job
- The opening signals what the chapter is about
- The closing lands something meaningful or practical

Paragraph Logic

- Paragraphs have clear points
- Transitions guide the reader
- No sudden topic jumps

Definitions

- Key terms defined before heavy use
- Jargon explained or avoided
- Cultural terms clarified if needed, without being erased

Action Steps
For nonfiction:

- Steps are explicit
- Examples support the steps
- Instructions are not vague

For fiction/memoir:

- Motivations make sense
- Emotional beats land
- Scenes are oriented clearly in time and place

If clarity fails, the reader feels lost. Lost readers stop reading.

3) Credibility: Do I Sound Honest and Reliable?

Credibility is not only about facts. It is about how I present myself.

Even in fiction, credibility matters because the reader must trust the internal world.

My Credibility Checks

Tone Discipline

- I do not overpromise
- I do not exaggerate claims
- I do not sound uncertain where confidence is needed
- I do not sound arrogant where humility is needed

Evidence and Support

For nonfiction:

- Claims are supported by reasoning, experience, or references when appropriate
- I avoid sweeping claims that invite doubt
- I distinguish what I know from what I believe

For memoir:

- I remain faithful to emotional truth
- I avoid framing that feels unfair or revenge-driven

Respect for the Reader

- I do not insult the reader's intelligence
- I do not repeat unnecessarily
- I do not manipulate emotionally

A credible book earns good reviews even when readers disagree. A book that feels dishonest earns harsh reviews even if the topic is interesting.

4) Typos and Mechanics: Are There Obvious Defects?

Typos are not the most important thing in a book, but they are the fastest way to destroy trust. Readers do not forgive repeated surface errors.

My Typos and Mechanics Checks

- spelling errors
- missing words
- doubled words
- punctuation glitches
- inconsistent quotes
- inconsistent apostrophes

- repeated spaces
- wrong homophones (their/there)

I do not chase microscopic perfection. I eliminate the errors that make the book feel careless.

5) Layout: Does the Book Look and Navigate Like a Real Book?

Layout is not separate from editing. Layout is part of quality.

My Layout Checks

Print

- margins comfortable
- gutter sufficient
- headers/footers consistent
- page numbers correct
- chapter starts clean
- no awkward page breaks
- lists aligned properly
- tables readable
- images properly placed
- no widows and orphans where avoidable

Ebook

- TOC works
- links work
- headings show correctly in navigation
- reflow works across devices
- images display properly
- no strange line breaks from manual formatting

Layout errors are humiliating because they are visible immediately. They are also avoidable with a final gate.

One Last Read Method: Print Proof, Read-Aloud, and Spot-Check Pages

A checklist alone is not enough. I also need a final reading method that exposes what checklists miss.

My final read method has three parts. I do not always do all three for every book, but for my serious releases, I do.

1) Print Proof: The Physical Reality Test

If the book is going to print, I treat print proof as the truth test.

When I hold the proof, I check:

- readability (font size, spacing)
- margin comfort
- chapter openings
- visual flow
- cover colors and spine alignment
- any pages that look cramped
- places where layout makes a paragraph feel awkward

Print reveals errors my screen hides.

If I cannot order a proof, I simulate it:

- I review the print PDF at 100% size
- I zoom in and out to see overall layout
- I scroll slowly as if turning pages

But a physical proof remains the best method.

2) Read-Aloud: The Ear Test

The ear catches problems the eye ignores.

When I read aloud, I catch:

- awkward sentence rhythm
- missing words
- repeated words
- confusing phrases
- unnatural dialogue (fiction)
- overly long sentences
- tone shifts

I do not read the entire book aloud unless I have time. Instead, I read aloud strategically:

- first chapter (first impression)
- last chapter (final impression)
- one chapter from the middle (pacing test)
- sections where beta readers reported confusion
- my most important teaching sections (nonfiction)

A small read-aloud sample can reveal many errors quickly.

3) Spot-Check Pages: The Random Gate

A full read is ideal, but fatigue can hide errors. Spot-checking helps because it forces fresh attention.

My spot-check method:

- I choose 10 random pages from the formatted file.
- I check them slowly for layout consistency and typos.
- I choose 5 pages from the front matter and back matter.
- I choose 5 pages where lists, tables, or images appear.

Random checks catch recurring formatting problems that appear throughout the book.

If my random pages show repeated issues, I pause. I fix the source problem, not just the pages.

My "First 10 Pages" Rule

The first 10 pages carry the biggest trust weight.

If the reader sees multiple errors in the first 10 pages, they assume the whole book is like that.

So I do a dedicated check of:

- opening pages
- chapter one formatting
- heading consistency
- early typos
- early clarity

The first 10 pages are the trust gate.

Practice Section: I Sign Off Only When I Can Answer: "Would I Buy This?"

This practice is not emotional. It is practical.

Before I publish, I must answer one question honestly:

Would I buy this?

Not would I buy it because I wrote it. Would I buy it if it were written by someone else, at this price, with this cover, with this description, and with this level of polish?

To answer honestly, I use a structured sign-off ritual.

Step 1: I Pretend I Am the Reader

I open the book as if I did not write it.

I look at:

- cover
- title/subtitle
- table of contents
- first chapter
- one middle chapter
- last chapter
- back matter

Then I ask:

- Does this feel professional?
- Does it feel easy to read?
- Does it feel trustworthy?

Step 2: I Rate Five Areas From 1 to 5

I rate:

- **Content value:** Does it deliver something meaningful?
- **Clarity:** Would a reader understand without struggle?
- **Consistency:** Does it hold together cleanly?
- **Professional polish:** Would errors embarrass me?
- **Packaging:** Does the cover and layout feel credible?

If any area scores below 4, I do not publish yet. I fix what is weak.

This simple scoring prevents me from publishing in a tired state.

Step 3: I Identify "Embarrassment Triggers"

I ask a blunt question:

- What would embarrass me if a serious reader pointed it out?

Common embarrassment triggers:

- obvious typos early in the book
- broken table of contents links
- inconsistent chapter headings
- misaligned cover text
- confusing description that overpromises
- contradictions in timeline or terms

If I can identify these triggers, I can fix them before they become public reviews.

Step 4: I Sign the Release Decision

I literally write a sign-off note, even if only for myself:

- "I have completed the quality gate. I approve this version for publication."

This may sound dramatic, but it changes my mindset. It turns publishing into a deliberate act rather than an impulsive click.

In indie publishing, discipline is a competitive advantage.

My Pre-Publish Checklist (Copy and Use)

Below is my full pre-publish checklist, combining reader trust and final gate steps. This is the checklist I would keep near my desk.

A) Reader Trust Checklist

- Consistency: names, terms, timeline, POV, tense
- Clarity: chapter purpose, transitions, definitions, orientation
- Credibility: honest tone, no overpromising, fair framing

- Typos: spelling, missing words, doubled words, punctuation
- Layout: headings, lists, tables, images, TOC, page numbers

B) Format-Specific Final Checks

Print

- Trim size correct
- Margins and gutter correct
- Page numbers correct
- Widows/orphans minimized
- Cover spine aligned
- Proof PDF reviewed carefully or print proof ordered

Ebook

- TOC links work
- Navigation works
- Reflow clean on multiple device views
- Links in back matter work
- No weird formatting glitches

C) Final Read Method

- First 10 pages checked carefully
- One middle chapter checked
- Last chapter checked
- Key sections read aloud
- 10 random pages spot-checked
- Front and back matter checked

D) Final Sign-Off Question

- Can I honestly say: "Would I buy this?"

If yes, I publish.
If no, I fix what makes the answer "no."

Closing Thought for Chapter 13

Indie publishing gives me freedom, but it also gives me responsibility. The final quality gate is how I respect that responsibility.

A reader buys trust, not just words. Trust is built through consistency, clarity, credibility, clean mechanics, and professional layout. A final proof after formatting protects the real product the reader will experience.

And the final question keeps me honest:

Would I buy this?

If I can answer yes, I publish with confidence. If I cannot, I do not rush. I fix it. Because publishing is not only about finishing. It is about shipping something I am proud to stand behind.

BACK MATTER

Final Note

If you remember only one thing from this book, let it be this: **editing is not a personality trait. It is a practice.** Some people seem naturally gifted at writing cleanly, but the truth is simpler and more hopeful. Professional-quality books are built by repeatable decisions, not by rare talent.

When I say "editing," I do not mean hunting commas or obsessing over grammar until I lose my mind. I mean the full discipline of turning raw material into something a reader can trust. I mean shaping meaning, tightening structure, strengthening clarity, and protecting consistency. I mean removing distractions so the reader can receive what I truly intended to give.

A draft is honest, but a draft is not finished. A draft is me thinking on paper. Editing is me respecting the reader.

I want you to remember that quality is not an event. Quality is a system. It has stages and gates. It has checklists and style sheets. It has time built into it. And it has humility built into it, because it accepts that I do not see everything the first time.

That is why the pass system matters. It keeps me from polishing paragraphs that should be moved. It keeps me from fixing surface issues while deeper issues remain. It gives me a map. It gives me order. It gives me peace while I work. When I edit in passes, I stop panicking and start building.

I also want you to remember that growth as an author is not only about writing more. It is about writing better with fewer wasted hours. Every book teaches me. Every edit reveals patterns. Every revision shows me where I need discipline, where I need stronger structure, and where my voice shines when it is not buried under clutter.

A strong author does not become strong by avoiding mistakes. A strong author becomes strong by turning mistakes into method.

If you keep publishing, you will face the same crossroads again and again:

- Do I rush, or do I respect the process?
- Do I publish "good enough," or do I publish something I can stand behind?
- Do I hide from feedback, or do I use it to build skill?
- Do I gamble with trust, or do I protect it?

I cannot make those choices for you. But I can tell you the outcome.

Readers forgive many things, but they do not forgive carelessness for long. When they trust you, they follow you. When they trust you, they buy your next book without fear. When they trust you, they recommend you. And trust is built in the quiet places most authors skip: the second pass, the style sheet, the proof after formatting, the one last read, the clean cover, the honest description.

So keep growing. Keep learning your patterns. Keep building your system. Keep improving your passes. And remember that your goal is not to produce a perfect book. Your goal is to produce a trustworthy book.

That kind of book changes your future.

Copies

If you want to use *The Editor's Guide 101* in a group setting, training, workshop, classroom, writing circle, or organizational program, you can request bulk copies and usage support.

Bulk Orders

Bulk orders are available for:

- Schools, colleges, and training centers
- Churches and community programs
- NGOs, youth groups, and literacy initiatives
- Publishing teams and writing collectives
- Corporate communications and staff training programs

Trainings and Workshops

Workshops and training sessions can be adapted to your needs, including:

- Self-editing systems for authors and teams
- Manuscript cleanup and style sheet building
- Editing levels and how to hire editors wisely
- Formatting checks for print and ebook publishing
- Publishing hygiene for KDP and product listings

How to Order and Request Support

Send a message with the subject line: **"Bulk Order / Training Request"** and include:

- Your name and organization
- Country and city
- Number of copies requested
- Intended use (training, workshop, classroom, organization distribution)
- Desired delivery timeline
- Any training or speaking request details (if applicable)

Contact:
Email: **[Your Email Here]**
Website: **[Your Website Here]**

If you prefer, you can also request an invoice and a short proposal outlining pricing, delivery options, and training scope.

Leave a Review

If this book helped you, I would appreciate an honest review. Reviews help other indie authors find practical books that save them time, money, and frustration.

If you are not sure what to write, you can use one of these prompts:

1. **What problem did this book help you solve in your editing process?**
2. **What is one method or checklist you used that improved your manuscript immediately?**
3. **Who would you recommend this book to, and why?**

Thank you for reading, and thank you for supporting indie authors.

About the Author

I am an indie author focused on helping writers publish books readers trust. My work is built around simple systems that remove guesswork from the self-publishing process, especially in editing, clarity, structure, and professional packaging. I write to help you move from draft to finished book with confidence, using repeatable passes, clean checklists, and practical publishing hygiene so you can build a catalog you are proud to stand behind.

If you want to go further, take what you learned here and apply it to one chapter today. Editing becomes easier when it becomes a habit.

www.ingramcontent.com/pod-product-compliance
Lightning Source LLC
Chambersburg PA
CBHW022341290526
45786CB00014B/2136